URBAN
TRAILS
EASTSIDE

URBAN
TRAILS

EASTSIDE

Bellevue · Issaquah Alps
Redmond · Snoqualmie Valley

CRAIG ROMANO

MOUNTAINEERS
BOOKS

MOUNTAINEERS BOOKS is dedicated to the exploration, preservation, and enjoyment of outdoor and wilderness areas.

1001 SW Klickitat Way, Suite 201, Seattle, WA 98134
800-553-4453, www.mountaineersbooks.org

Printed in China
Distributed in the United Kingdom by Cordee, www.cordee.co.uk
First edition, 2019

Copyeditor: Emily Barnes
Design: Jen Grable
Layout: Twozdai Hulse
Cartographer: Erin Greb Cartography

Cover Photo: *Trail along the Tolt River at Tolt River-John McDonald Park (Trail 55)*
Frontispiece: *Preston Snoqualmie Trail (Trail 56)*

All photographs by the author unless credited otherwise

Library of Congress Cataloging-in-Publication Data is on file for this title at https://lccn.loc.gov/2018053636

Mountaineers Books titles may be purchased for corporate, educational, or other promotional sales, and our authors are available for a wide range of events. For information on special discounts or booking an author, contact our customer service at 800-553-4453 or mbooks@mountaineersbooks.org.

Printed on FSC©-certified materials

ISBN (paperback): 978-1-68051-028-7
ISBN (ebook): 978-1-68051-029-4

CONTENTS

BOTHELL, KENMORE, KIRKLAND & WOODINVILLE

BELLEVUE, REDMOND & NEWCASTLE

MERCER ISLAND

ISSAQUAH & SAMMAMISH

ISSAQUAH ALPS
COUGAR MOUNTAIN

TRAILS AT A GLANCE

Trail and/or Park	Distance	Walk	Hike	Run	Kids	Dogs*
BOTHELL, KENMORE, KIRKLAND & WOODINVILLE						
1. Brightwater Center	3 miles of trails	•		•	•	•
2. Sammamish River Trail	10 miles one-way	•		•	•	•
3. Tolt Pipeline Trail	14 miles one-way	•	•	•	•	•
4. Saint Edward State Park	more than 9 miles of trails	•	•	•	•	•
5. Big Finn Hill Park	9.5 miles of trails	•	•	•	•	•
6. O. O. Denny Park	2 miles of trails	•	•		•	
7. Juanita Bay and Juanita Beach Parks	2 miles of trails	•		•	•	•
8. Watershed Park	2 miles of trails	•		•	•	•
9. Cross Kirkland Corridor	5.75 miles one-way	•		•	•	•
BELLEVUE, REDMOND & NEWCASTLE						
10. Bridle Trails State Park	28 miles of trails		•	•	•	•
11. PSE Trail	4 miles one-way	•		•		•
12. Farrel-McWhirter Farm Park	more than 2 miles of trails	•	•	•	•	•
13. Redmond Watershed Preserve	more than 8 miles of trails	•	•	•	•	
14. Redmond Ridge Trails	more than 20 miles of trails	•	•	•	•	•
15. Marymoor Park	more than 5 miles of trails	•		•	•	•
16. Mercer Slough Nature Park	more than 7 miles of trails	•	•	•	•	•
17. Wilburton Hill Park and Bellevue Botanical Garden	more than 3 miles of trails	•	•	•	•	•

*May be limited to portions of hike

Trail and/or Park	Distance	Walk	Hike	Run	Kids	Dogs*
18. Kelsey Creek Farm Park	more than 2.5 miles of trails	•	•	•	•	•
19. Lake Hills Greenbelt	3 miles of trails	•	•	•	•	•
20. Weowna Park	2.5 miles of trails		•	•	•	•
21. Robinswood Park	more than 2 miles of trails	•		•	•	•
22. Lakemont Park	2.5 miles of trails	•	•	•	•	•
23. Lewis Creek Park	3 miles of trails	•	•	•	•	•
24. May Creek Trail	up to 5.9 miles roundtrip		•	•	•	•
25. Coal Creek Natural Area	5.5 miles of trails		•	•	•	•
MERCER ISLAND						
26. Luther Burbank Park	more than 2 miles of trails	•		•	•	•
27. Mercerdale Park	1.5 miles of trails	•		•		•
28. Pioneer Park	7 miles of trails	•	•	•	•	•
ISSAQUAH & SAMMAMISH						
29. Lake Sammamish State Park	more than 5 miles of trails	•	•	•	•	•
30. East Lake Sammamish Trail	10.4 miles one-way			•	•	•
31. Evans Creek Preserve	3.5 miles of trails		•	•	•	•
32. Soaring Eagle Regional Park	more than 12 miles of trails	•	•	•	•	•
33. Beaver Lake and Hazel Wolf Wetlands Preserves	more than 3 miles of trails	•	•		•	•
34. Grand Ridge Park	more than 12 miles of trails		•	•	•	•

*May be limited to portions of hike

Trail and/or Park	Distance	Walk	Hike	Run	Kids	Dogs*
ISSAQUAH ALPS: COUGAR MOUNTAIN						
35. De Leo Wall	4.8 miles roundtrip		•	•	•	•
36. Coal Creek Falls	2.5 miles roundtrip		•	•	•	•
37. Anti-Aircraft Peak Loop	4.4 miles roundtrip		•	•	•	•
38. Big Tree Ridge	4.4 miles roundtrip		•	•	•	•
39. Wilderness Peak Loop	3.9 miles roundtrip		•	•	•	•
ISSAQUAH ALPS: SQUAK MOUNTAIN						
40. Bullitt Fireplace	3.6 miles roundtrip		•	•	•	•
41. Margaret's Way and Debbie's View	7 miles roundtrip		•	•	•	•
42. May Valley Loop	7.2 miles roundtrip		•	•	•	•
43. East Ridge	8 miles roundtrip		•	•	•	•
ISSAQUAH ALPS: TIGER MOUNTAIN						
44. Tradition Lake Plateau	more than 8 miles of trails	•	•	•	•	•
45. West Tiger Mountain	up to 7.8 miles roundtrip		•		•	•
46. Tiger Mountain Trail (TMT)	16 miles one-way		•	•	•	•
47. Poo Poo Point	up to 9 miles roundtrip		•	•	•	•
48. West Tiger Railroad Grade	7.2 miles roundtrip		•	•	•	•
49. Middle Tiger Mountain	10 miles roundtrip		•	•	•	•

*May be limited to portions of hike

Trail and/or Park	Distance	Walk	Hike	Run	Kids	Dogs*
ISSAQUAH ALPS: TAYLOR & RATTLESNAKE MOUNTAINS						
50. Taylor Mountain Forest	more than 20 miles of trails		•	•	•	•
51. Rattlesnake Ledge and Mountain Traverse	up to 10.7 miles one-way		•	•		•
SNOQUALMIE VALLEY						
52. Ring Hill Forest	2.7 miles of trails		•	•	•	•
53. Lower Snoqualmie Valley Trail	18.8 miles one-way	•	•	•	•	•
54. Moss Lake Natural Area	about 3 miles of trails	•	•	•	•	•
55. Tolt River–John MacDonald Park	more than 12 miles of trails	•	•	•	•	•
56. Preston-Snoqualmie Trail	11 miles roundtrip	•	•	•	•	•
57. Snoqualmie Falls	1.4 miles roundtrip	•			•	•
58. Meadowbrook Farm	more than 3 miles of trails	•		•	•	•
59. Tollgate Farm Park	1.5 miles of trails	•		•		•
60. Upper Snoqualmie Valley Trail	9.4 miles one-way	•	•	•	•	•

*May be limited to portions of hike

INTRODUCTION
TRAILS FOR FUN AND FITNESS IN YOUR BIG BACKYARD

LET'S FACE IT: WHETHER YOU'RE a hiker, walker, or runner, life can get in the way when it comes to putting time in on the trail. Far too often, it's hard for most of us to set aside an hour—never mind a day, or even longer—to hit the trails of our favorite parks and forests strewn across the state. But that doesn't mean we can't get out on the trail more frequently. Right in and near our own communities are thousands of acres of parks and nature preserves containing hundreds of miles of trails. And we can visit these pocket wildernesses, urban and urban-fringe parks and preserves, greenbelts, and trail corridors on a whim—for an hour or two without having to drive far. Some of these places we can even visit without driving at all—hopping on the bus instead—lessening our carbon footprint while giving us more time to relax from our hurried schedules.

Urban Trails: Eastside focuses on the myriad of trails, parks, and preserves within the urban, suburban, and rural fringe areas in Bellevue and adjacent Eastside cities, as well as Mercer Island and the Snoqualmie River Valley to North Bend. You'll find trails to old-growth forests, lakeshores, riverfronts, shorelines, wildlife-rich wetlands, rolling hills, small mountains, scenic vistas, meadows, historic sites, and vibrant neighborhoods and communities. While often we equate hiking trails with the state's wildernesses and forests, there are plenty of areas of natural beauty and accessible trails in the midst of our population centers. The routes included here are designed to show you where you can go for a good run, long walk, or quick hike right in your own backyard.

This guide has two missions. One is to promote fitness and get you outside more often! A trip to Mount Rainier, North Cascades, or Olympic National Parks can be a major undertaking for many of us. But a quick outdoor getaway to a local park or trail can be done almost anytime—before work, during a lunch break, after work, or when we don't feel like fighting traffic and driving for miles. And all of these trails are available year round, so you can walk, run, or hike every day by utilizing the trails within your own neighborhood. If you feel you are not getting outside enough or getting enough exercise, this book can help you achieve a healthier lifestyle.

Mission number two of this guide is to promote the local parks, preserves, and trails that exist within and near our urban areas. More than 4.8 million people (2.2 million in King County alone) call the greater Puget Sound area home. While conservationists continue to promote protection of our state's large, roadless wild corners—and that is still important—it's equally important that we promote the preservation of natural areas and develop more trails and greenbelts right where people live. Why? For one thing, the Puget Sound area contains unique and threatened ecosystems that deserve to be protected as much as our wilder remote places. And we need to have usable and accessible trails where people live, work, and spend the majority of their time. Urban trails and parks allow folks to bond with nature and be outside on a regular basis. They help us cut our carbon footprint by giving us access to recreation without burning excessive gallons of fuel to reach a destination. They make it easier for us to commit to regular exercise programs, giving us safe and

Family friendly hiking at Evans Creek Preserve (Trail 31)

agreeable places to walk, run, and hike. And urban trails and parks also give disadvantaged populations—folks who may not have cars or the means to travel to one of our national parks or forests—a chance to experience nature and a healthy lifestyle too. As the greater Puget Sound area continues to grow in population and becomes increasingly more crowded and developed, it is all the more important that we support the expansion of our urban parks and trails.

So get out there, get fit, and have fun! And don't forget to advocate for more trails and parks.

Next page: *Thundering Snoqualmie Falls (Trail 57)*

HOW TO USE
THIS GUIDE

THIS EASY-TO-USE GUIDE PROVIDES YOU with enough details to get out on the trail with confidence, while leaving enough room for your own personal discovery. I have walked, hiked, or run every mile of the trails described here, and the directions and advice are accurate and up to date. Conditions can and do change, however, so make sure you check on the status of a park or trail before you go.

THE DESTINATIONS

This book includes sixty destinations, covering trails in and around Bellevue, Kirkland, Redmond, Newcastle, Sammamish, Woodinville, Issaquah, Snoqualmie, and North Bend—as well as the Issaquah Alps. Each one begins with the park or trail name followed by a block of information detailing the following:

Distance. Here you will find roundtrip mileage (unless otherwise noted) if the route describes a single trail, or the total mileage of trails within the park, preserve, or greenway if the route gives an overview of the destination's trail system. Note that while I have measured most of the trails in this book with GPS and have consulted maps and governing land agencies, the distance stated may not always be exact—but it'll be pretty darn close.

Elevation gain. For individual trails, elevation gain is for the *cumulative* difference on the route (and return), meaning not only the difference between the high and low points on the trail but also for all other significant changes in elevation along the way. For destinations where multiple routes are given, as in a trail network within a park, the elevation gain applies to the trail with the most vertical rise on the route.

High point. The high point is the highest elevation of the trail or trail system described. Except for a couple of the Issaquah Alps hikes, almost all of the trails in the book are at a relatively low elevation, ensuring mostly snow-free winter access.

Difficulty. This factor is based not only on length and elevation gain but also on the type of tread and surface area of a trail or trails. Most of the trails in this book are easy or moderate for the average hiker, walker, or runner. Depending on your level of fitness, you may find the trails more or less difficult than described.

Fitness. This description denotes whether the trail is best for hikers, walkers, or runners. Generally, paved trails will be of more interest to walkers and runners, while rough, hilly trails will appeal more to hikers. Of course you are free to hike, walk, or run (unless running is specifically prohibited) on any of the trails in this book.

Family-friendly. Here you'll find notes on a trail's or park's suitability for children and any cautions to be aware of, such as cliffs, heavy mountain-bike use, and so on. Some trails may be noted as suitable for jogging strollers or as ADA accessible.

Dog-friendly. This denotes whether dogs are allowed on the trail and what regulations (such as leashed and under control) apply.

Amenities. The featured park's amenities can include privies, drinking water, benches, interpretive signs and displays, shelters, learning centers, and campgrounds, to name a few.

Contact/maps. Here you'll find the trail's or park's managing agency. All websites and phone numbers for trail and park managers or governing agencies can be found in the Resources section at the end of the book. These websites

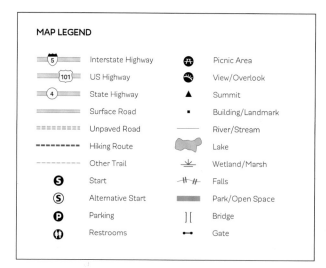

will often direct you to trail and park maps; in some cases, a better or supplemental map is noted (such as Green Trails).

Before You Go. This section notes any fees or permits required, hours the park or preserve is open (if limited), closures, and any other special concerns.

GPS. GPS coordinates in degrees and decimal minutes (based on the WGS84 datum) are provided for the main trail-head, to help get you to the trail.

Next, I describe how to get to the trailhead via your own vehicle or by public transport if available.

GETTING THERE. Driving: Provides directions to the trail-head—generally from Bellevue, the nearest freeway exit, or a major road. Often I state directions from more than one desti-nation and for more than one trailhead—and I provide parking information. **Transit:** If the trailhead is served by public trans-portation, this identifies the bus agency and line.

EACH HIKE begins with an overview of the featured park or trail, highlighting its setting and character, with notes on the property's conservation history.

GET MOVING. This section describes the route or trails and what you might find on your hike, walk, or run, and may note additional highlights beyond the trail itself, such as points of historical or natural interest.

GO FARTHER. Here you'll find suggestions for making your hike, walk, or run longer within the featured park—or perhaps by combining this trip with an adjacent park or trail.

PERMITS, REGULATIONS, AND PARK FEES

Many of the trails and parks described in this book are managed by county and city parks departments, requiring no permits or fees. Destinations managed by Washington State Parks and the Washington Department of Natural Resources (DNR) require a day-use fee in the form of the Discover Pass (www.discoverpass.wa.gov) for vehicle access. A Discover Pass can be purchased per vehicle per day or annually for up to two vehicles. You can purchase the pass online, at many retail outlets, or from a state park office to avoid the handling fee. Each hike in this book clearly states if a fee is charged or a pass is required.

Regulations, such as whether dogs are allowed or a park has restricted hours or is closed for certain occasions (such as during high fire danger or for wildlife management), are clearly spelled out in the trail information blocks.

ROAD AND TRAIL CONDITIONS

In general, trails change little year to year. But change can occur, and sometimes quickly. A heavy storm can wash out sections of a trail or access road in moments. Wind storms can blow down multiple trees across trails, making paths impassable. Lack of adequate funding is also responsible for trail neglect and degradation. For some of the wilder destinations in this book, it is wise to contact the appropriate land manager after a significant weather event to check on current trail and road conditions.

Peaceful wanderings at Meadowbrook Farm (Trail 58)

On the topic of trail conditions, be appreciative of the thousands of volunteers who donate tens of thousands of hours to trail maintenance each year. The Washington Trails Association (WTA) alone coordinates more than 150,000 hours of volunteer trail maintenance each year. But there is a need for more. Our trail systems face ever-increasing threats, including lack of adequate trail funding. Consider joining one or more of the trail and conservation groups listed in the Resources section.

OUTDOOR ETHICS

Strong, positive outdoor ethics include making sure you leave the trail (and park) in as good a condition as you found it—or even better. Get involved with groups and organizations that safeguard, watchdog, and advocate for land protection. And get on the phone and keyboard and let land managers and public officials know how important protecting lands and trails is to you.

All of us who recreate in Washington's natural areas have a moral obligation and responsibility to respect and protect our natural heritage. Everything we do on the planet has an impact—and we should strive to have as little negative impact as possible. The **Leave No Trace** Center for Outdoor Ethics is an educational, nonpartisan, nonprofit organization that was developed for responsible enjoyment and active steward-ship of the outdoors. Their program helps educate outdoor enthusiasts about their recreational impacts and recom-mends techniques to prevent and minimize such impacts. While geared toward backcountry use, many Leave No Trace (LNT) principles are also sound advice for urban and urban-fringe parks too, including: plan ahead, dispose of waste prop-erly, and be considerate of other visitors. Visit www.lnt.org to learn more.

TRAIL ETIQUETTE

We need to be sensitive not only to the environment surrounding our trails but to other trail users as well. Some of the trails in this book are also open to mountain bikers and equestrians. When you encounter other trail users, whether they are hikers, runners, bicyclists, or horseback riders, the only hard-and-fast rule is to follow common sense and exer-cise simple courtesy. With this Golden Rule of Trail Etiquette firmly in mind, here are other things you can do during trail encounters to make everyone's trip more enjoyable:

- **Observe the right-of-way.** When meeting bicyclists or horseback riders, those of us on foot should move off the trail. This is because hikers, walkers, and runners are more mobile and flexible than other users, making it easier for us to quickly step off the trail.
- **Move aside for horses.** When meeting horseback riders specifically, step off the downhill side of the trail unless the terrain makes this difficult or dangerous. In that case, move to the uphill side of the trail, but crouch down a bit

so you do not tower over the horses' heads. Also, make yourself visible so as not to spook the big beastie, and talk in a normal voice to the riders. This calms the horses. If walking with a dog, keep your buddy under control.

- **Stay on trails.** Don't cut switchbacks, take shortcuts, or make new trails; all lead to erosion and unsightly trail degradation.

- **Obey the rules specific to the trail or park you are visiting.** Many trails are closed to certain types of use, including dogs and mountain bikes. Some trails are bike only—don't walk on them.

- **Keep dogs under control.** Trail users who bring dogs should have their dog on a leash or under very strict voice-command at all times. And if leashes are required, then this *does* apply to you. Many trail users who have had negative encounters with dogs (actually with the dog owners) on the trail are not fond of, or are even afraid of, encountering dogs. Respect their right *not* to be approached by your darling pooch. A well-behaved leashed dog, however, can certainly help warm up these folks to a canine encounter. And always pack out your dog's poop and discard of it properly.

- **Avoid disturbing wildlife.** Observe from a distance, resisting the urge to move closer to wildlife (use your telephoto lens). This not only keeps you safer but also prevents the animal from having to exert itself unnecessarily to flee from you.

- **Take only photographs.** Leave all natural features and historic artifacts as you found them for others to enjoy.

- **Never roll rocks off of trails or cliffs.** Gravity increases the impact of falling rocks exponentially, and you risk endangering lives below you.

- **Mind the music.** Not everyone (almost no one) wants to hear your blaring music. If you like listening to music while you run, hike, or walk, wear headphones and respect other trail users' right to peace and quiet—and to listen to nature's music.

HUNTING

Nearly all of the destinations in this book are closed to hunting. However, a couple of areas are open to hunting and are so noted. While using trails in areas frequented by hunters, it is best to make yourself visible by donning an orange cap and vest. If hiking with a dog, your buddy should wear an orange vest too.

BEARS AND COUGARS

Washington harbors healthy populations of black bears in many of the parks and preserves along the urban fringe. If you encounter a bear while hiking, you'll usually just catch a glimpse of its bear behind. But occasionally the bruin may actually want to get a look at *you*.

To avoid an un-*bear*-able encounter, practice bear-aware prudence: Always keep a safe distance. Remain calm, do not look a bear in the eyes, speak in a low tone, and do not run from it. Hold your arms out to appear as big as possible. Slowly move away. The bear may bluff-charge—do not run. Usually the bear will leave once he perceives he is not threatened. If he does attack, fight back using fists, rocks, trekking poles, or bear spray if you are carrying it.

Our state also supports a healthy population of *Felix concolor*. While cougar encounters are extremely rare, they do occur—even occasionally in parks and preserves on the urban fringe. In 2018 a bicyclist was fatally attacked by a cougar outside of North Bend. Cougars are cats—they're curious. They may follow hikers but rarely (almost never) attack adult humans. Minimize contact by not hiking or running alone and by avoiding carrion. If you do encounter a cougar, remember the big cat is looking for prey that can't or won't fight back. Do not run, as this may trigger its prey instinct. Stand up and face it. If you appear aggressive, the cougar will probably back down. Wave your arms, trekking poles, or a jacket over your head to appear bigger, and maintain eye contact. Pick up children and small dogs and back away slowly if you can do so safely, not taking your eyes off of it. If it attacks, throw things at it. Shout loudly. If it gets close, whack it with your trekking pole, fighting back aggressively.

WATER AND GEAR

While most of the trails in this book can be enjoyed without much preparation or gear, it is always a good idea to bring water, even if you're just out for a quick walk or run. Even better, carry a small pack with water, a few snacks, sunglasses, and a rain jacket.

A NOTE ABOUT SAFETY

Safety is an important concern in all outdoor activities. No guidebook can alert you to every hazard or anticipate the limitations of every reader. Therefore, the descriptions of roads, trails, routes, and natural features in this book are not representations that a particular place or excursion will be safe for your party. When you follow any of the routes described in this book, you assume responsibility for your own safety. Under normal conditions, such excursions require the usual attention to traffic, road and trail conditions, weather, terrain, the capabilities of your party, and other factors. Because many of the lands in this book are subject to development and/or change of ownership, conditions may have changed since this book was written that make your use of some of these routes unwise. Always check for current conditions, obey posted private property signs, and avoid confrontations with property owners or managers. Keeping informed on current conditions and exercising common sense are the keys to a safe, enjoyable outing.

—*Mountaineers Books*

THE TEN ESSENTIALS

If you are heading out for a longer adventure—perhaps an all-day hike in the Issaquah Alps—pack the **Ten Essentials**, items that are good to have on hand in an emergency:

1. **Navigation.** Carry a map of the area you plan to be in and know how to read it. A cellphone or GPS unit is good to have along too.

2. **Headlamp.** If caught out after dark, you'll be glad you have a headlamp or flashlight so you can follow the trail home.

3. **Sun protection.** Even on wet days, carry sunscreen and sunglasses; you never know when the clouds will lift, and you can easily sunburn near water.

4. **First-aid supplies.** At the very least, your kit should include bandages, gauze, scissors, tape, tweezers, pain relievers, antiseptics, and perhaps a small manual.

5. **Knife.** A pocketknife or multitool can come in handy, as can basic repair items such as nylon cord, safety pins, a small roll of duct tape, and a small tube of superglue.

6. **Fire.** While being forced to spend the night out is not likely on these trails, a campfire could provide welcome warmth in an emergency, with matches kept dry in a zip-lock bag.

7. **Emergency shelter.** This can be as simple as a garbage bag or a rain poncho that can double as an emergency tarp.

8. **Nutrition.** Pack a handful of nuts or sports bars for emergency pick-me-ups.

9. **Hydration.** Bring enough water to keep you hydrated, and for longer treks consider a means of water purification.

10. **Insulation.** Storms can and do blow in rapidly. Carry raingear, wind gear, and extra layers.

TRAILHEAD CONCERNS

By and large, our parks and trails are safe places. Common sense and vigilance, however, are still in order. This is true for all trail users, but particularly so for solo ones. Be aware of your surroundings at all times. Let someone know when and where you're headed out.

Sadly, car break-ins are a common occurrence at some of our parks and trailheads. Absolutely under no circumstances leave anything of value in your vehicle while out on the trail. Take your wallet and cellphone with you. A duffel bag on the back seat may contain dirty T-shirts, but a thief may think there's a laptop in it. Save yourself the hassle of returning to a busted window by not giving criminals a reason to clout your car.

Vagrants and substance abuse are concerns at several of our urban parks as well. It's best not to wander off trail, and if you come upon a homeless encampment, leave the area and report the situation to the authorities. Be aware of needles, human waste, and other hazardous debris around such encampments. Parks and trails where this is a serious concern have been omitted from this book.

No need to be paranoid, though, for our trails and parks are fairly safe places. Just use a little common sense and vigilance while you're out and about. Most importantly, be safe and enjoy the thrill of discovery and exercise on the trails in this book. They exist for our enjoyment, and for the enjoyment of future generations of hikers, runners, walkers, and cyclists. Happy Trails!

Next page: *Quiet, forested trail in King County's Big Finn Hill Park (Trail 5)*

BOTHELL, KENMORE, KIRKLAND & WOODINVILLE

The cities of Kenmore (population 25,000) and Kirkland (population 90,000) sit along the northeastern shore of Lake Washington, while the cities of Bothell (population 50,000) and Woodinville (population 15,000) sit along the Sammamish River, which drains into the lake. Like other Eastside communities, these four cities have seen explosive growth over the past few decades, transforming sleepy downtowns into major hubs—and rural woodlands into housing developments. They're home to high-tech and retail centers, top-notch medical facilities, and several universities. But also within the tidy rows of homes and steel-and-glass complexes lie tracts of farmland, large woodlots, and some of the last large tracts of undeveloped Lake Washington shoreline. Parks and conservation easements protect them while trails traverse them. Several long-distance trails also tie these and other communities together.

1   Brightwater Center

DISTANCE:	3 miles of trails
ELEVATION GAIN:	Up to 150 feet
HIGH POINT:	275 feet
DIFFICULTY:	Easy
FITNESS:	Runners, walkers
FAMILY-FRIENDLY:	Yes, and jogging stroller–friendly
DOG-FRIENDLY:	On leash
AMENITIES:	Restrooms, benches, interpretive displays
CONTACT/MAPS:	Brightwater Center (King County)
BEFORE YOU GO:	Open dawn to dusk
GPS:	N 47°47.458', W 122°08.461'

GETTING THERE

Driving: From Bellevue follow I-405 north for 9.7 miles. Take exit 23 and then follow State Route 522 east for 2.7 miles. Take exit for SR 9 north and turn left onto SR 9 (Woodinville-Snohomish Road). Proceed for 0.7 mile and turn right into Brightwater Center complex. Continue for 0.1 mile and turn left into parking area for the trailhead.

Not a park, preserve, or greenbelt, the Brightwater Center is a wastewater treatment plant—and a visual, ecological, and recreational treat! This center features 70 acres of restored riparian habitat, public displays of art, and aesthetically pleasing storm water retention and filtration ponds. Enjoy traversing the grounds on 3 miles of well-groomed, interconnecting trails. Watch for birds and amphibians, admire a cascading creek, and marvel at this state-of-the-art facility.

GET MOVING

Actually located in Snohomish County in the old railroad whistle-stop of Grace, Brightwater is owned and managed by King County and is just minutes from downtown Woodinville.

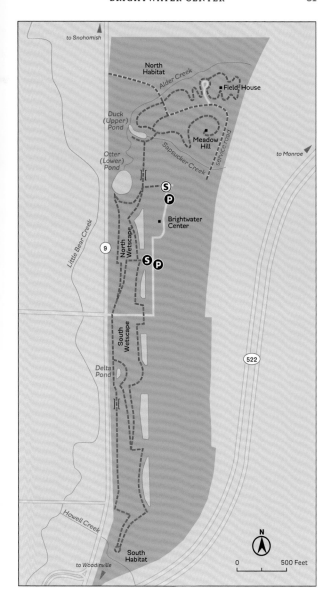

Near the Delta Pond in the South Wetscape

Despite a controversial history and hefty price tag ($1.8 billion), even its critics would have to admit that Brighwater is impressive. A 13-mile-long tunnel allows the facility to release treated water into Puget Sound. Unlike most wastewater treatment plants, you won't be treated to a noxious odor here. You can learn all about the facility and other important water issues at the center's environmental education and community center (open Monday through Thursday, 10:00 AM to 4:00 PM).

From either parking area, pick up the trail system and let the roaming begin. You can make a long loop, a figure eight, or amble willy-nilly. The trail system is classified into four parts: the North Habitat and North Wetscape, and the South Habitat and South Wetscape. The center's access road divides the property north and south.

The wetscapes are primarily open and manicured with retention ponds. The habitat areas are more natural with flowing creeks and groves of mature timber. There are several bridges and boardwalks along the way and a couple of salmon observation points—one at the Otter (Lower) Pond and one at the Duck (Upper) Pond. The Field House loop will give you a good workout with a rolling route that includes a couple of short, steep sections. Meadow Hill will allow you to gain some elevation too—and there's even a little view of the Little Bear Creek Valley. The trail distance from end (Howell Creek overlook) to end (Meadow Hill or the Field House) is 1.1 miles. Out and back makes 2.2 miles. Add a few extra loops, and you can easily hike or run 3 to 4 miles here.

GO FARTHER

Not too far from Brightwater Center is Woodinville's small Rotary Community Park (19518 136th Avenue NE). Here you can walk a pretty little loop complete with a boardwalk along the Little Bear Creek.

2 Sammamish River Trail

DISTANCE:	10 miles one-way
ELEVATION GAIN:	Minimal
HIGH POINT:	40 feet
DIFFICULTY:	Easy
FITNESS:	Walkers, runners, cyclists
FAMILY-FRIENDLY:	Yes, and jogging stroller–friendly; but be aware of heavy bicycle use
DOG-FRIENDLY:	On leash
AMENITIES:	Restrooms, benches, water, interpretive signs
CONTACT/MAPS:	King County Parks
GPS:	N 47°45.015', W 122°12.610'

GETTING THERE

Driving: The trail can be accessed from several parks with parking and facilities, including the following: *Red Brick Road Park (Bothell):* From Bellevue, follow I-405 north and take exit 23. Then follow State Route 522 west for 2 miles. Turn left onto 96th Avenue NE and proceed 0.1 mile to park on your right. *Wilmot Gateway Park (Woodinville):* From Bellevue, follow I-405 north and take exit 23. Follow SR 522 east for 0.8 mile. Then turn right onto 131st Avenue NE and proceed 0.3 mile to park on your right. There's more parking on your left at the Woodinville Sports Fields. *Sixty Acres Park:* From Bellevue, follow I-405 north and take exit 20B. Then turn right onto NE 124th Street and drive 1.3 miles. Next turn right onto Willows Road and continue for 0.5 mile. Then turn left onto NE 116th Street (York Road) and drive 0.6 mile to park on your left. *Marymoor Park (Redmond):* See directions for Marymoor Park (Trail 15).

Transit: *Red Brick Road Park (Bothell):* King County Metro lines 312, 342, 372. *Wilmot Gateway Park (Woodinville):* King County Metro line 236. *Marymoor Park (Redmond):* See directions for Marymoor Park (Trail 15).

A key linchpin in the region's paved, long-distance trail network, the Sammamish River Trail is treasured by cyclists. But walkers and runners love it too. Paralleling the Sammamish River for 10 miles, this nearly level path passes through vibrant communities, a multitude of parks, and across some of the last agricultural lands remaining on the Eastside. Explore it piecemeal, or arrange for a shuttle (or bus ride) and do the entire trail in one sweep.

GET MOVING

While any section of this 10-mile-long trail makes for a good walk or run, the four best places to access it are the four places listed above in Getting There. Below is a brief description of the entire trail from north to south.

The Sammamish River Trail actually begins a short distance east from Red Brick Road Park. You'll need to walk a short distance on the Burke-Gilman Trail (see *Urban Trails: Seattle*) to access it. But first check out the historic displays and remnant stretch of Red Brick Road. From 1912 to 1915,

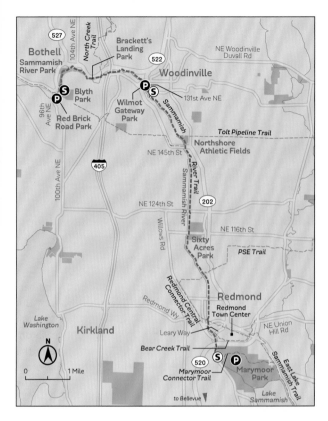

Greek and Italian immigrants laid red bricks over the old Military Road (commissioned by Secretary of War Jefferson Davis in the late 1850s) between Seattle and Bothell to help facilitate travel. The road became the first "paved" route to Seattle around the north end of Lake Washington. And that old golf course to the south is now Bothell's newest park and will remain a big green spot on the Sammamish River.

Now walk the Burke-Gilman Trail east through a tunnel beneath 96th Avenue NE, and in 0.2 mile reach a junction at milepost 20. Here the Burke-Gilman continues straight on

Cottonwoods and Lombardy poplars line the trail

a trestle across the Sammamish River, reaching Blyth Park (parking, restroom, and alternative start) before ending a short distance farther on Riverside Drive. You want to take the Sammamish River Trail left and begin your journey following this waterway upriver.

The path soon crosses the river and traverses a lovely greenbelt of parks on the river's bend in downtown Bothell. There's a path leading left across the river to the Park at Bothell Landing and a path leading right to Blyth Park. At 0.7 mile (from trail's start) come to the Sammamish River Park (parking). Then dart under 102nd Avenue NE and follow the river, soon crossing it once more and coming to Brackett's Landing Park at 1.4 miles. The trail then follows a residential road shoulder for a short distance before resuming as a path.

At 1.6 miles the North Creek Trail departs left (see Go Farther). Continue right, passing under noisy I-405 and then traversing a large, grassy expanse. Pass beneath a trestle that will hopefully soon be part of the Cross Kirkland Corridor extension (see Trail 9), and reach the attractive Wilmot Gateway Park (parking, restrooms, water) at 2.9 miles.

The trail now heads south, soon breaking out into open country. Before the 1960s the river was quite curvy, but it has since been altered into a channel bordered by levees. The trail pretty much utilizes those levees for its level course. The way is lined with stately Lombardy poplars as it traverses remnant farmland and thriving vineyards. At 4.4 miles the Tolt Pipeline Trail (see Trail 3) takes off east. Shortly afterward reach the Northshore Athletic Fields (parking and restrooms).

The way then darts under NE 145th Street, passes some condominiums, and then continues through a long stretch of open fields. When the skies are clear, Mount Rainier looms in the distance. The way ducks under NE 124th Street and comes to Sixty Acres Park (parking, restrooms, and water) at 6.6 miles.

The paved path continues south, while a paralleling soft-surface path now runs along the river on the east side all the way to Leary Way. As the trail gets closer to bustling Redmond, passing residences, businesses, and civic buildings, expect a lot more foot traffic on the path. There are some sculptures, gardens, and interpretive displays along the way too if you want to slow your pace down and check them out. At 7.8 miles come to a junction with the PSE Trail (see Trail 11). At 8.8 miles reach a junction with the new Redmond Central Connector Trail. The path passes under its trestle—but stairs and a side trail connect with this paved path, which you can follow east 1 mile to Redmond Town Center.

The Sammamish River Trail continues south, ducking under Redmond Way and then coming to a junction with the paved Bear Creek Trail at 9.2 miles. This path follows alongside Bear Creek for 1.7 miles, ending at NE Union Hill Road and connecting to the Redmond Central Connector Trail along the way. The Sammamish River Trail crosses the river, scoots under Leary Way and SR 520, and terminates at sprawling Marymoor Park (see Trail 15) at 10 miles.

GO FARTHER

Consider checking out some of the trails that branch off the Sammamish River Trail. At the trail's southern terminus, you can follow the 1.5-mile paved Marymoor Connector Trail (see Trail 15) to the 11-mile paved East Lake Sammamish Trail (see Trail 30). In Redmond, you can leave the trail for a 2-mile loop via the Bear Creek and Redmond Central Connector Trails. And in Bothell, you can follow the paved North Creek Trail for 1.1 miles through the UW Bothell and Cascadia College campuses and a restored wetland, complete with observation decks. The trail continues north just beyond the I-405 exchange and will eventually connect with the section in Mill Creek.

3 Tolt Pipeline Trail

DISTANCE:	14 miles one-way
ELEVATION GAIN:	Up to 3000 feet
HIGH POINT:	550 feet
DIFFICULTY:	Easy to strenuous
FITNESS:	Walkers, runners, hikers, cyclists
FAMILY-FRIENDLY:	Yes, but be aware of bikes and horses
DOG-FRIENDLY:	On leash
AMENITIES:	Restrooms, water, picnic tables at Northshore Athletic Fields
CONTACT/MAPS:	King County
GPS:	N 47°43.994', W 122°08.678'

GETTING THERE

Driving: The trail can be accessed from several road crossings with limited parking. Here are the best access points for the two main trail sections: *Northshore Athletic Fields (NAF):* From Bellevue, follow I-405 north and take exit 20B. Then turn right onto NE 124th Street and drive 0.6 mile. Turn left onto Slater Avenue NE, which becomes 132nd Avenue NE, and

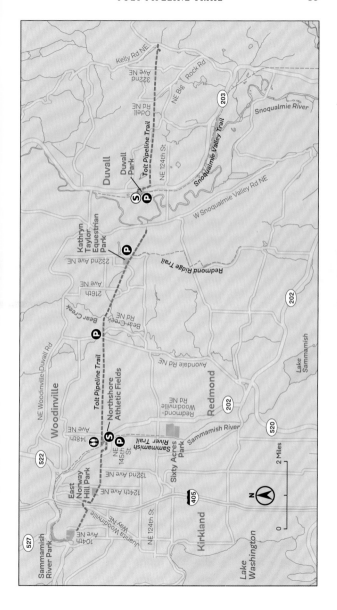

drive 1.4 miles. Then turn right onto NE 143rd Street (which becomes 137th Place NE, then NE 145th Street and State Route 202) and continue for 1.1 miles to a traffic circle and entrance (north) to parking and the trailhead. *Duvall Park:* From Bellevue, follow I-405 north for 1 mile. Then take the exit for SR 520 east. After 6.3 miles SR 520 becomes Avondale Road NE. Continue straight for 1 mile and bear right onto NE Novelty Hill Road. After 4.7 miles, bear left onto W. Snoqualmie Valley Road NE. After 0.3 mile turn right onto NE 124th Street and drive 1 mile to a traffic circle. Exit north on the traffic circle and follow SR 203 for 0.8 mile to parking at Duvall Park on your left.

Transit: *Brickyard Road Park and Ride (Bothell):* King County Metro lines 236, 238, 255, 535. *Duvall Park:* King County Metro line 629. *Avondale Road NE:* King County Metro lines 232, 931.

Primarily a gravel service road along the Tolt (water) Pipeline right-of-way, this trail does have its fans. Trail runners like to train on its series of short, steep hills. And many local walkers take to sections for quiet reprieves from much busier trails nearby. It is also good for tying together other trails. And finally, there are some scenic stretches along the way, including views out to the Cascades and Olympics.

GET MOVING

The entire trail is 14 miles long, but not contiguous. It consists primarily of two stretches. The trail's midsection is the most popular, with several access points. The Northshore Athletic Fields (privies and plenty of parking) is the best place to access the western reaches of the trail. Duvall Park is the best access point for the trail's eastern stretch.

From the Northshore Athletic Fields Trailhead, you can head east or west. The westernmost reach, however, crosses several busy roads and is appealing primarily to area residents

Runner enjoying the Tolt Pipeline Trail's hilly terrain

who use it for short walks and runs. If you want to check it out, head west on the trail—here a paved path paralleling NE 145th Street. Immediately cross the Sammamish River. The path then bends north to parallel the Redmond-Woodinville Road NE, coming to the pipeline at 0.6 mile. The pipeline, originating from water drawn from the South Fork Tolt River, supplies the greater Seattle area with 30 percent of its water.

Now using extreme caution—there's no crosswalk—cross the very busy Redmond-Woodinville Road NE. Then, on the pipeline gravel right-of-way, climb steeply. You'll pass an exposed section of the pipeline as you climb about 350 feet. Then gradually descend, reaching busy 124th Avenue NE (another potentially dangerous crossing) at 1.6 miles. The way then rolls along, passing by Bothell's East Norway Hill Park. At 2.2 miles reach 116th Avenue NE.

From here the trail follows sidewalks north on 116th Avenue NE to busy Juanita Woodinville Way NE to 115th Avenue NE—then resumes as a trail once more. The final stretch gains about 200 feet up Norway Hill, ending in a residential area on 104th Avenue NE at 3.4 miles.

To head east on the trail from the Northshore Athletic Fields, begin by first walking north on the paved Sammamish

River Trail for 0.3 mile. Then head east on the gravel Tolt Pipeline Trail, coming to 148th Avenue NE (crosswalk signal) at 0.6 mile from the trailhead. Cross the road and steeply climb. The way dips a little while it climbs more than 500 feet. Traverse a semi-rural landscape of forest, home sites, and horse farms. Enjoy views west to the Olympics. At 2.6 miles come to the first of several trails traversing the Brook Trails Estates.

At 3.5 miles, cross Avondale Road NE (crosswalk signal, parking). The trail soon crosses Bear Creek Road NE and Bear Creek and then begins a long uphill stretch, gaining more than 300 feet. At 5 miles come to 216th Avenue NE (large trailhead parking). Then continue on a fairly gentle stretch, coming to a trail junction at 5.8 miles. Here a path leads south to Redmond Ridge (see Trail 14). At 6.1 miles come to 232nd Avenue NE near the Kathryn Taylor Equestrian Park. Plenty of parking here and access to the paved Redmond Ridge Trail. The Tolt Pipeline Trail continues east for another 0.9 mile, descending steeply more than 200 feet to terminate at NE 133rd Street.

To reach the lightly used eastern section of the Tolt Pipeline Trail, park at Duvall Park and carefully cross busy SR 203. Then walk up a dirt road directly across from the park and near a Seattle Public Utilities facility. On an upward march, the road bends left at 0.3 mile and transitions to trail. Still climbing and passing through forest, the trail reaches NE Big Rock Road (parking) at 2 miles. Then still climbing, but more gradually, the trail reaches Odell Road NE (parking) at 2.8 miles.

The trail then traverses more forest and gradually descends, with one short uphill stretch. At 3.8 miles cross 322nd Avenue NE (parking). From here the way drops, losing more than 200 feet. Enjoy good views to the Cascades from a bluff before reaching a short switchback at a ravine. At 4.6 miles the trail terminates at Kelly Road NE (parking).

4

Saint Edward State Park

DISTANCE:	More than 9 miles of trails
ELEVATION GAIN:	Up to 500 feet
HIGH POINT:	450 feet
DIFFICULTY:	Easy to moderate
FITNESS:	Hikers, runners, walkers, cyclists
FAMILY-FRIENDLY:	Yes, but some trails open to mountain bikes
DOG-FRIENDLY:	On leash
AMENITIES:	Restrooms, benches, playground, picnic tables
CONTACT/MAPS:	Washington State Parks
BEFORE YOU GO:	Discover Pass required; park open 8:00 AM to dusk
GPS:	N 47°44.074', W 122°15.401'

GETTING THERE

Driving: From Bellevue, follow I-405 north for 6 miles. Take exit 20A and turn left onto NE 116th Street. Continue west for 1.4 miles. Then continue straight onto Juanita Drive NE and drive for 3.9 miles. Turn left onto NE 145th Street and proceed into Saint Edward State Park. Continue for 0.5 mile to parking areas and the trailhead.

From Kenmore, follow 68th Avenue NE (which becomes Juanita Drive NE) for 1.8 miles south. Then turn right onto NE 145th Street and proceed into Saint Edward State Park. Continue for 0.5 mile to parking areas and the trailhead.

Transit: King County Metro line 234 stops at NE 153rd Place and Juanita Drive NE near the park's northeast corner.

Saint Edward State Park contains the largest undeveloped stretch of shoreline on Lake Washington. A former Catholic seminary, this lovely hilltop and lakeside retreat contains historic Romanesque buildings and more than 9 miles of trails. Hike or run down lush ravines and up forested ridges and

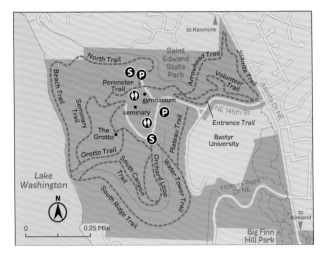

hillsides. And stroll along more than 3000 feet of wild Lake Washington lakeshore—one of the many blessings this popular park has to offer.

GET MOVING

This beautiful state park has several facets. One is its undeveloped, heavily forested ravines, hillsides, and lakeshore. Another is its playfields and playground—one of the largest and most impressive in the state. And yet another is the park's historic grounds and structures. From the trailhead you can immediately head for the forest and soak up the park's wild side. However, if this is your first visit, you may want to head first on the 0.75-mile Perimeter Trail, which winds along the bluff top encircling the former seminary buildings.

Several interpretive signs line the way. The imposing main seminary building was built during the Great Depression under the tutelage of Seattle's first bishop, Edward O'Dea. Remarkably, he raised $100,000 and secured a loan for $200,000 during this difficult time to help facilitate its construction. Saint Edward would become the first fully accredited seminary in the country, but in 1976 it closed for good due to declining enrollment. Washington State Parks (WSP) acquired the property a year later. Bastyr College lies several buildings away from the main seminary building, which WSP and a developer are currently working to restore. It is being redeveloped as a lodge and conference center, complete with a spa and restaurant. While the developers are retaining the structure's historical integrity, some park users are fearful the lodge will compromise the integrity of the park.

After you walk the Perimeter Trail, start exploring the myriad of paths branching off it. There are several ways to get to Lake Washington—and several ways to make a loop trip out of it. The easiest way is the 0.6-mile Seminary Trail, which utilizes an old service road. It is also open to mountain bikes.

The most difficult and longest way to the lake is via the 0.3-mile Water Tower Trail to the 1-mile South Ridge Trail. You'll gain a little elevation along the way before steeply dropping to the lake. The 0.5-mile South Canyon Trail is exceptionally pretty, dropping into a creek-fed ravine. You can return via the

Hikers watch a pair of kayakers in Lake Washington.

nearby 0.4-mile Grotto Trail, which delivers you to the stone-built Grotto, a former place of worship that is now a popular wedding spot.

My favorite route is via the 0.6-mile North Trail, which winds down a ravine nestling a small creek. From there you can follow the 0.4-mile Beach Trail, traveling along beautiful Lake Washington shoreline. Now choose your return to the bluff top—my preference is the South Ridge Trail. You can then call it a hike or extend your wandering with some of the upland trails. These trails traverse mature forest and also form many loops. A grand circuit around the park is a little more than 3 miles.

GO FARTHER

Near the park's main entrance road, you can follow a trail leading to several other trails in the park's quiet southeast corner. Two of these trails lead to adjoining Big Finn Hill Park (see Trail 5) where nearly 10 more miles of trails await your boots.

5   Big Finn Hill Park

DISTANCE:	9.5 miles of trails
ELEVATION GAIN:	Up to 200 feet
HIGH POINT:	460 feet
DIFFICULTY:	Easy to moderate
FITNESS:	Hikers, runners, walkers, cyclists
FAMILY-FRIENDLY:	Yes, but be aware of heavy mountain-bike use on some trails
DOG-FRIENDLY:	On leash
AMENITIES:	Restrooms, benches, sports fields, mountain-bike skills areas
CONTACT/MAPS:	King County Parks
BEFORE YOU GO:	Parking area on NE 138th Street gated at dusk
GPS:	N 47°43.458', W 122°14.114'

Well-groomed trail through a stand of stately firs

GETTING THERE

Driving: From Bellevue, follow I-405 north for 6.5 miles. Then take exit 20B and turn left onto Totem Lake Boulevard NE. Continue for 0.7 mile and turn left onto NE 132nd Street. Follow this road (which becomes NE 131st Way and then 90th Avenue NE) for 2.1 miles. Then turn left onto NE 136th Street, which becomes NE 137th Street, for 0.5 mile. Next turn right onto 84th Avenue NE, and after 0.1 mile turn left onto NE 138th Street. Drive 0.2 mile to parking and the trailhead.

From Kenmore, follow 68th Avenue NE, which becomes Juanita Drive NE, for 2.5 miles south. Then turn left onto NE 138th Street and continue for 0.2 mile to parking and the trailhead.

Transit: King County Metro lines 234, 244

Adjacent to popular Saint Edward State Park (see Trail 4), the Big Finn Hill King County Park also contains miles of interconnecting trails. But unlike the state park, Big Finn Hill's trails tend to be quieter and not on the radar of hikers and runners not from the immediate area. Built primarily for mountain bikers, the trails here also make excellent running routes. And despite being on Big Finn Hill (named for a big hill or a big Finn?), most of the trails are pretty gentle with little elevation gain, making them perfect for easy strolls.

GET MOVING

Juanita Drive NE bisects Big Finn Hill Park's 220 acres. East of that arterial, the park is developed with playfields, play equipment, big parking lots, and access to two schools. The trails in this section are not too interesting—they skirt buildings, roads, and developed areas of the park. The section of the park on the west side of Juanita Drive NE is much more alluring, with attractive forest, a hillier topography, and a larger trail network. There is a trail that connects the two sections. Use caution crossing busy Juanita Drive NE. You can skip the western section of the park entirely by parking (road shoulder) on NE 138th Place near its junction with Juanita Drive NE.

The park's trail system is confusing, as it is poorly marked. The online map, however, is pretty accurate. If you are good at map reading it will come in handy. Junctions are numbered—and there are currently sixty-nine of them. However, only a handful of them are signed—so again, the system is confusing. The park isn't very large, though, so if you get lost, it will only be for a short period. Do be aware of mountain bikers on the trails and shy away from trails better designed for them—the ones with challenge courses and bike skill areas.

In the park's eastern section, you can hike or run about 2 miles by following trails along the periphery. There is a large beaver pond you can hike around, but note that you will have to walk a short section on 84th Avenue NE to complete the loop. There are some large cottonwoods in the vicinity, but generally the forest here is pretty scrappy.

In the park's western section, you can put in quite a few more miles. Near the parking areas along NE 138th Place is a major trailhead complete with kiosk. Here the Maintenance Access Trail heads directly down the middle of this park section, terminating at NE 132nd Street. This trail is about a half mile long and connects to many other trails. It also passes through an old orchard with a picnic table. If you hike along the periphery of this section, you'll rack up about 1.3 miles. On the north side of NE 138th Place, two trails of about 0.2 mile each head north, connecting to trails within Saint

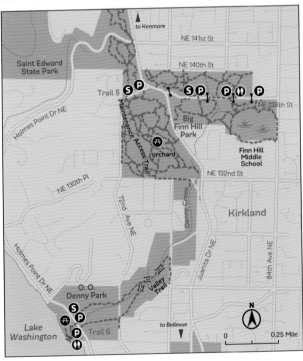

Edward State Park (see Trail 4). You'll know you reached the park when the forest suddenly transitions to older and statelier trees.

GO FARTHER

Continue hiking or running into Saint Edward State Park (see Trail 4), and you'll have enough miles of trails before you to hike all day or to train for an ultra-run.

6   O. O. Denny Park

DISTANCE:	2 miles of trails
ELEVATION GAIN:	Up to 290 feet
HIGH POINT:	320 feet
DIFFICULTY:	Easy to moderate
FITNESS:	Hikers, walkers
FAMILY-FRIENDLY:	Yes
DOG-FRIENDLY:	On leash
AMENITIES:	Restrooms, benches, picnic shelter, play equipment, interpretive signs
CONTACT/MAPS:	City of Kirkland Parks and Community Services
GPS:	N 47°42.590', W 122°14.988'

GETTING THERE

Driving: From Bellevue, follow I-405 north for 6 miles. Then take exit 20A and turn left onto NE 116th Street. Continue west for 1.4 miles. Then continue straight on Juanita Drive NE for 2 miles. Next, turn left onto 76th Place NE (which becomes Holmes Point Drive NE) and drive 1.1 miles to trailhead parking on your right.

From Kenmore, follow 68th Avenue NE, which becomes Juanita Drive NE, for 2.2 miles south. Then turn right onto Holmes Point Drive NE and continue for 1.9 miles to trailhead parking on your left.

There are just a couple of miles of trails located within this small park occupying a lush emerald ravine on the shores of Lake Washington (see Trail 5 for map). But those 2 miles are loaded with natural beauty, including a salmon-spawning creek and what was once one of the largest Douglas firs in King County. And the history this park packs in is bountiful, including a link to the city of Seattle's founders.

GET MOVING

O. O. Denny Park protects one of the last undeveloped ravines and stretches of shoreline remaining on massive Lake Washington. When the park was established, however, much of the area was still pretty wild. The park is named for Orion Orvil Denny, the first non-Native boy born in Seattle. Denny's father was Arthur Denny, one of Seattle's founders.

O. O. Denny Park was once Denny's country estate, Klah-anie. Upon his death in 1916, his widow willed the estate to

Denny Creek flowing with maple leaves

the City of Seattle. In 1922 it became a park, and in 1926 it became a camp for Seattle children. In the 1930s the Civilian Conservation Corps (CCC) built and improved the park's facilities and trails. In the late 1960s, camping ceased at the park. Seattle continued to own it, but King County Parks managed it. In 2001, a budget shortfall led to a creative partnership. Today the Finn Hill Park and Recreation District manages the property for the City of Seattle.

Denny Park is actually only 46 acres in size. But it borders a section of Big Finn Hill Park (see Trail 5) as well as private conservation land. The park's trails continue into these adjoining green swaths, allowing for longer roaming. Two trails depart from the large parking lot, forming a 1-mile loop through the ravine housing Denny Creek.

The southern stretch climbs a bit above the ravine and intersects an old road, now used as a trail. The road-trail then descends to cross Denny Creek on an old CCC-built stone bridge near some former home sites. Just beyond the crossing is a trail junction. The loop continues left, traversing a grove of impressive old-growth trees, including one 600-year-old Douglas fir known as Sylvia. Sylvia once stood more than 250 feet tall, until the Inaugural Day Storm of 1993 toppled her top. The loop trail continues, passing the easy-to-miss Valley Trail before returning to the parking lot. The lightly traveled Valley Trail heads 0.5 mile and climbs about 300 feet to 72nd Avenue NE.

The trail heading upstream from the junction near the stone bridge is a delight and a little bit of a calorie burner. It starts off easy enough, passing an old shed that looks like it came out of a 1970s horror flick. The trail then makes three crossings of Denny Creek on attractive bridges surely to delight children and photographers. Beyond the third crossing, the trail steeply climbs out of the ravine, reaching 76th Avenue NE about 0.4 mile from the junction.

Be sure to also cross Holmes Point Drive NE and walk the short Beach Park Trail. Check out two more bridges across Denny Creek and a beautiful stretch of beach and lakeshore. Seattle's Sand Point lies nearly directly across the lake. When the sky is clear, your eyes will be drawn southward for a breathtaking view of Mount Rainier hovering above the lake.

7 Juanita Bay and Juanita Beach Parks

DISTANCE:	2 miles of trails
ELEVATION GAIN:	50 feet
HIGH POINT:	70 feet
DIFFICULTY:	Easy
FITNESS:	Walkers, runners
FAMILY-FRIENDLY:	Yes, and jogging stroller–friendly
DOG-FRIENDLY:	On leash
AMENITIES:	Restrooms, benches, picnic shelter, play equipment, interpretive signs
CONTACT/MAPS:	City of Kirkland Parks and Community Services
BEFORE YOU GO:	Parks open dawn to dusk; restrooms closed November–March
GPS:	N 47°41.745', W 122°12.654'

GETTING THERE

Driving: From Bellevue, follow I-405 north for 6 miles. Then take exit 20A and turn left onto NE 116th Street. Continue west for 1.4 miles. Then turn left onto 98th Avenue NE (or continue straight for 0.3 mile on Juanita Drive NE for the Juanita Beach Park on your left) and drive south 0.7 mile to the Juanita Bay Park Trailhead and parking on your right.

Transit: King County Metro lines 234, 236, 255

Once bustling with ships and nearly filled in by an ambitious and environmentally unenlightened developer, today Juanita Bay is one of the prettiest and best spots for birdwatching on Lake Washington. Juanita Bay and Juanita Beach Parks contain a couple of miles of trails that will take you along and upon the bay. Literally walk on water, taking to the parks' boardwalks, docks, and an old causeway. Sunsets here are supreme—you can watch the evening light dance upon sparkling lake waters and Seattle's shimmering skyscrapers.

GET MOVING

These two parks are not contiguous, but they are close. You can visit them individually or together via a short and safe sidewalk connection.

From the parking area at Juanita Bay Park, pick up a paved path and start winding downhill across manicured slopes. Come to a junction. The paved path left leads across the grassy open area to 20th Avenue W. There are two paths that divert north off it, leading to boardwalks at the bay's edge. The one farther west is particularly pleasing—it leads to Nelson Point, which cradles a quiet cove that usually flourishes with avian and amphibian activity.

The paved path heading right from the first junction is where most folks venture. This trail soon connects to an old roadway, which turns north and makes a nearly half-mile straight line cut across the bay on an old causeway. The road was decommissioned in the 1970s and now is one of the most beloved and scenic trails on Lake Washington.

Take your time, pausing at all of the interpretive panels along the way explaining the area's natural and human history. The bay was once bustling with vessels, but when the lake was lowered in 1916 due to the Montlake Cut, it became too shallow for docking. Years later a developer began filling in the bay with cedar bark, sawdust, and soil for a golf course. Thankfully the soggy golf course was eventually abandoned, and this entire area became a beloved park. Volunteers, government officials, and conservationists have worked hard since trying to restore much of the park's 3000-foot shoreline.

The trail crosses five plant communities along the bay. This diversity in vegetation is responsible for the plethora—more than a hundred species—of wildlife that resides here.

The causeway trail ends at 98th Avenue NE. From here, follow a sidewalk along this road to Juanita Drive NE. Then turn left to reach Juanita Beach Park, which lies 0.25 mile away from Juanita Bay Park. At 22 acres, this park is much smaller than Juanita Bay Park (110 acres) and much more developed. But it contains 1000 feet of shoreline and a

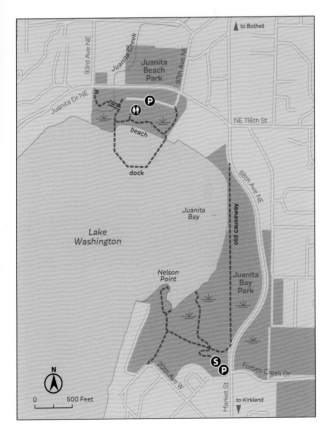

Juanita Bay glows in evening light

0.25-mile enclosed dock that is a delight to walk—especially during sunsets. Combine the dock with the promenade along the beach and the short nature trail near Juanita Creek, and you'll have a nice add-on walk from Juanita Bay Park. You probably noticed the large parking lot here too—a good option when the parking lot is full at Juanita Bay Park.

8   Watershed Park

DISTANCE:	2 miles of trails
ELEVATION GAIN:	Up to 225 feet
HIGH POINT:	430 feet
DIFFICULTY:	Easy to moderate
FITNESS:	Walkers, runners
FAMILY-FRIENDLY:	Yes
DOG-FRIENDLY:	On leash
AMENITIES:	Privy, benches
CONTACT/MAPS:	City of Kirkland Parks and Community Services
BEFORE YOU GO:	Park open dawn to dusk
GPS:	N 47°38.997', W 122°11.611'

GETTING THERE

Driving: From Bellevue, follow I-405 north and take exit 14 to State Route 520 west. Then immediately take the exit for 108th Avenue NE. Turn right onto 108th Avenue NE and head north for 0.7 mile. Then turn right onto NE 45th Street. Continue for 0.1 mile to trailhead, where NE 45th Street intersects with 110th Avenue NE. Park on the road shoulder.

Transit: King County Metro line 255 stops at the corner of 108th Avenue NE and NE 45th Street.

Not to be confused with Redmond's popular Watershed Preserve (Trail 13), this little wooded oasis in bustling Kirkland is not well known. Enjoyed by neighbors who regularly walk their dogs or go for a run here, Kirkland's Watershed

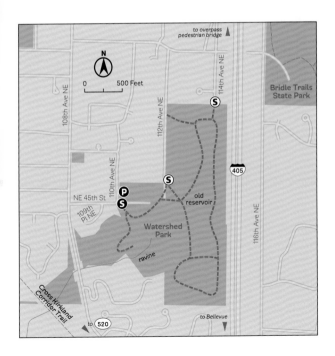

Tall Douglas firs in the Kirkland Watershed

Park doesn't see too many other visitors. Enjoy checking out this former city water supply by exploring old structures and wandering through groves of big trees, catching a few good glimpses out over Lake Washington.

GET MOVING

From the unassuming trailhead, follow a wide trail and soon come to a junction. The way right steeply drops 0.2 mile to a spring-fed creek in a ravine graced with big, old firs. There are remnants of pipelines here from when this watershed provided water for a much smaller Kirkland. The trail left steeply climbs beneath a canopy of tall maples and cottonwoods. It passes by a trailhead on 112th Avenue NE before coming to a junction at a forest opening at 0.2 mile. Here on a bluff above the ravine are the remains of a small reservoir.

A 0.9-mile loop trail takes off from this spot. It's fairly level with just a few little dips. Most of the way is mature forest with small wetland pockets. Other than the buzz of nearby I-405 and the occasional peek through the trees at the Seattle and Bellevue skylines, you'll feel that you're farther out in the countryside. There are two spurs that branch off this loop—one leading to 112th Avenue NE and one leading to a trailhead on 114th Avenue NE.

The 0.9-mile loop also intersects a smaller 0.3-mile loop that circles around a large depression left behind from freeway construction. This open bowl is choked with dreaded Scotch broom, but volunteers and parks personnel have recently been busy trying to eradicate this invasive pox on the land. Hopefully someday it will be adorned in native vegetation.

GO FARTHER

You can easily combine a run or walk here with the nearby Bridle Trails State Park (see Trail 10). From the 114th Avenue NE Trailhead, walk north on 114th Avenue NE through quiet neighborhoods, following sidewalks and a path where the road is disjointed. Reach NE 60th Street and turn right to cross I-405 on an overpass pedestrian bridge. Enjoy excellent views west to the Olympics. Continue east on NE 60th Street and carefully cross 116th Avenue NE. Then, at 0.7 mile from Watershed Park, pick up a trail on your right in Bridle Trails State Park. Follow it a short distance to the Raven Loop Trail. Then head out for as many miles as you want to add on!

9 | Cross Kirkland Corridor

DISTANCE:	5.75 miles one-way
ELEVATION GAIN:	Up to 200 feet
HIGH POINT:	180 feet
DIFFICULTY:	Easy
FITNESS:	Walkers, runners, cyclists
FAMILY-FRIENDLY:	Yes, and jogging stroller–friendly; but be aware of bicycle use
DOG-FRIENDLY:	On leash
AMENITIES:	Benches, water, interpretive signs, restrooms at adjacent parks
CONTACT/MAPS:	City of Kirkland
GPS:	N 47°38.648', W 122°11.664'

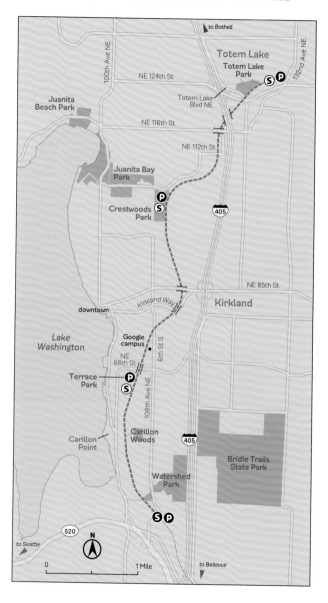

GETTING THERE

Driving: The trail can be accessed from several parks with parking and facilities, including the following: *South Kirkland Park and Ride:* Follow I-405 north and take exit 14 to State Route 520 west. Then immediately take the exit for 108th Avenue NE. Turn right onto 108th Avenue NE and head north for 0.2 mile. Turn left onto NE 37th Court and immediately turn right into park and ride. *Terrace Park:* From Bellevue, follow I-405 north and take exit 17. Turn left onto 116th Avenue NE and soon afterward left onto NE 70th Place. Follow this road (which becomes NE 68th Place) for 0.8 mile. Then turn left onto 104th Avenue NE and continue 0.1 mile to the park and parking on your left. *Crestwoods Park Athletic Fields:* From Bellevue, follow I-405 north and take exit 18. Then turn right onto NE 85th Street and drive 0.6 mile. Next turn right onto 6th Street and continue for 0.6 mile. Bear left onto 15th Avenue and immediately turn right onto 5th Place. After 0.1 mile turn right onto 18th Avenue. Soon turn left into the park and parking area. *Northern Trailhead:* From Bellevue, follow I-405 north and take exit 20B for NE 124th Street. Bear right onto NE 124th Street and continue 0.5 mile. Then turn left onto 128th Lane NE and drive 0.1 mile to trailhead parking on your right.

Transit: *South Kirkland Park and Ride:* King County Metro lines 234, 235, 249, 255, 540, 981, 986. *Terrace Park:* King County Metro line 238 stops on NE 68th Place. *Northern Trailhead:* King County Metro lines 235, 236, 237 stop on Totem Lake Boulevard NE near trail.

Run or walk part or all of this wonderful soft-surfaced rail trail traversing Kirkland from south to north. Traveling mostly through quiet residential and light industrial areas—as well as a few greenbelts—the trail is surprisingly quiet and scenic. Enjoy wide views out over Lake Washington to Seattle and the Olympic Mountains, as well as glimpses of little Totem Lake.

A forested greenbelt along the Cross Kirkland Corridor

GET MOVING

Opened in 2015, this 5.75-mile trail owned by the City of Kirkland was once part of the Lake Washington Belt Line railway. Built in 1904, the 42-mile rail line extended from Renton to Snohomish and was used primarily to transport coal and timber. Rail use changed over the years, and by 2007 the last trains used the line. Now city and county planners, as well as trail advocates, are working on reopening more than 16 miles of the former line as the Eastside Rail Corridor Trail. This new trail will tie together existing trails, including the Sammamish River, Redmond Central Connector, 520, and I-90 Trails. In the meantime, give the Cross Kirkland Corridor (CKC) a look.

Following is a brief description of the trail from south to north. The trail begins on the Kirkland–Bellevue border on 108th Avenue NE. Gently climbing, it traverses a hillside above Yarrow Bay on Lake Washington while skirting quiet neighborhoods. Enjoy sweeping views over Lake Washington to Seattle and the Olympic Mountains. At 1 mile reach a trailhead on NE 55th Street, where it's a short walk east to Carillon Woods Park.

The CKC then bends northeast, passing several secondary trailheads. At 1.6 miles it reaches Terrace Park and a major trailhead. Then it cross NE 68th Street on a trestle; at 2 miles come to another major trailhead at the Google campus. Here pass a playground, benches, a caboose, and some sand volleyball courts.

The trail then crosses busy 6th Street S. and continues up a forested corridor between residences and light industry. The trail makes a bridged crossing of busy Kirkland Way and ducks under busy NE 85th Street. At 3.5 miles it reaches Crestwoods Park with its playground, sports fields, and ample parking for trail access. Enjoy a nice forested stretch here; there are also some side trails (a few with steps) to explore if you feel like deviating from the main path.

The CKC then enters a busier area of businesses. It ducks under NE 116th Street, crosses 120th Avenue NE, and goes beneath I-405 before coming to NE 124th Street at 5.25 miles. Here you'll need to use crosswalks to cross a couple of busy arterials before returning to the rail corridor and traversing the small Totem Lake Park, a tiny little natural area in a sea of suburban sprawl. At 5.5 miles the trail reaches 128th Lane NE and the northern trailhead. The CKC continues another 0.25 mile to Slater Avenue NE, but there is no parking here.

GO FARTHER

From the southern trailhead, you can head south on a recently opened 1.3-mile section of the Eastside Rail Trail Corridor to 120th Avenue NE in Bellevue. A new section of this corridor also opened in 2018 in Newcastle.

Next page: Vine maple arches at Lewis Creek Park (Trail 23)

BELLEVUE, REDMOND & NEWCASTLE

The largest city on the Eastside and fifth-largest in the state, Bellevue (population 150,000) is also one of the region's top trail towns. Long a sleepy suburb wedged between Lakes Washington and Sammamish, the city is now an economic, cultural, and commercial center in its own right. It's ethnically and culturally diverse too, owing largely to its high-tech industries, which attract workers from around the country and the world.

Bellevue also contains one of the state's finest urban parks and trail systems. The city borders and contains large parks and preserves traversed and interconnected by miles of trails. Redmond (population 65,000), best known as the home to Microsoft, sits to the northeast of Bellevue. Beyond its bustling downtown and high-tech campuses, you'll find some of the best urban parks in the state—as well as some of the region's best-loved long-distance trails. To the south of Bellevue lies Newcastle (population 15,000), a mostly well-to-do residential suburb occupying land within an old coal mining district between Lake Washington and Cougar Mountain. Traces of the old town still exist within the city and its parks. And the city has recently been moving forward with building a trail system throughout the municipality.

10 Bridle Trails State Park

DISTANCE:	28 miles of trails
ELEVATION GAIN:	Up to 150 feet
HIGH POINT:	530 feet
DIFFICULTY:	Easy
FITNESS:	Hikers, runners
FAMILY-FRIENDLY:	Yes, but be alert for equestrians; horses have right-of-way
DOG-FRIENDLY:	On leash and kept under control
AMENITIES:	Privy, interpretive signs, picnic tables, equestrian facilities
CONTACT/MAPS:	Washington State Parks
BEFORE YOU GO:	Discover Pass required; park open winter 8:00 AM to dusk, summer 6:30 AM to dusk
GPS:	N 47°39.314', W 122°11.052'

GETTING THERE

Driving: From Bellevue, follow I-405 north and take exit 17. Turn right onto 116th Avenue NE and drive 0.9 mile. Then turn left into Bridle Trails State Park and proceed to the large parking area and trailhead.

A former state land grant property, Bridle Trails State Park was born during the Great Depression. The Lake Washington Saddle Club helped develop and maintain the park's excellent and sprawling trail network, and equestrians certainly use this park today in full force. But the park is open to pedestrians too, and it ranks as a favorite training ground for area trail runners. The terrain is gentle and the forest spectacular—including a large pocket of old-growth.

GET MOVING

At 482 acres, Bridle Trails State Park forms a huge greenbelt between the growing cities of Bellevue and Kirkland. Most of the park was logged in the early 1900s, and 160 acres of the original tract was sold to developers. But area residents, particularly equestrians, pushed for the creation of a state park. Trails and facilities were first developed during the Great Depression. The land eventually became a state park (deeded in 1992), only to be threatened with closure ten years later due to a state budget crisis. But through a negotiation with a newly formed citizens group, the Bridle Trails Park Foundation (which agreed to pay for half of the park's operating expenses), the park remains open.

The main trailhead is located next to the large arena and staging ground where horse shows are frequently held. Remember, equestrians have the right-of-way here—and

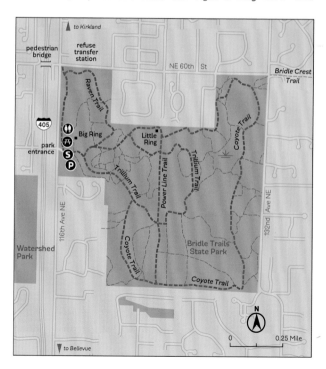

The trails are well-marked with icons.

dogs absolutely *must* be leashed. There are 28 miles of trails within the park, which can at first glance appear to be a spaghetti heap. But don't fret if you've never been here before and are worried about getting lost. There are three signed loops of varying distances within the park, which are wonderful for getting orientated. These three trails primarily utilize service roads but feel very much like trails. They are wide, smooth, and a blast to run. Most of the secondary trails are single track, and you can run or hike on them to your heart's content. Create your own loops, from short jaunts to ultra-ultra-distances!

All three signed loops originate from the same spot—a kiosk just east of the main parking lot. The Raven Trail is the shortest, at 1 mile, and it makes a loop in the park's northwest corner. The Trillium Trail is 1.7 miles long, and it makes a loop in the heart of the park. It traverses the oldest grove of trees in the park, passing by Douglas firs and western red cedars more than 250 years old. The Coyote Trail is 3.5 miles long and pretty much follows along the park's periphery, except for the northwest corner. It passes several pocket wetlands and includes a few little dips, breaking up a mostly level terrain.

GO FARTHER

From the park's northeast corner, you can follow the soft-surface Bridle Crest Trail for 1.2 miles east to the paved 520 Bike Trail. Then you can head north on that trail for 0.8 mile to the Sammamish River Trail (see Trail 2) and then keep going!

11 PSE Trail

DISTANCE:	4 miles one-way
ELEVATION GAIN:	Up to 800 feet
HIGH POINT:	325 feet
DIFFICULTY:	Easy to moderate
FITNESS:	Runners, walkers, cyclists
FAMILY-FRIENDLY:	Yes, but note trail shared with bikes and horses
DOG-FRIENDLY:	On leash
AMENITIES:	Restrooms, water available at Farrel-McWhirter Farm Park
CONTACT/MAPS:	King County Parks
BEFORE YOU GO:	Park open 7:00 AM to dusk
GPS:	N 47°41.865', W 122°04.908'

GETTING THERE

Driving: From Bellevue, follow I-405 north for 1 mile. Then take the exit for State Route 520 east. After 6.3 miles, SR 520 becomes Avondale Road NE. Continue straight on Avondale Road NE for 2.2 miles and turn right onto NE 116th Street. Then drive 0.7 mile and turn right onto 196th Avenue NE. After 0.3 mile, turn right into Farrel-McWhirter Farm Park and continue a short distance to trailhead parking.

Transit: King County Metro lines 224, 232 stop on Avondale Road NE. King County Metro lines 243, 244, 930 stop on Willows Road.

Hiker crossing the Sammamish River

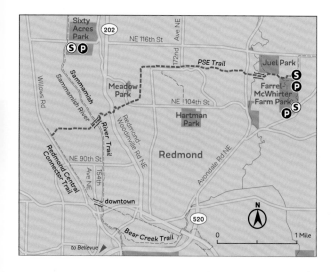

Also referred to as the Redmond Puget Power Trail, the PSE (Puget Sound Energy) Trail may indeed energize you. Yes, this path follows a powerline swath, but it also includes plenty of electrifying natural scenery along the way. Buzz through forest patches, wetlands, and rolling hills granting good views of distant Cascades peaks. The trail includes a lot of ups and downs too, assuring your heart rate gets a few jolts.

GET MOVING

The PSE Trail has two faces. The eastern 3.2 miles primarily consist of a wide, soft-surface service road with sections of single track. The western 0.8 mile is narrow, paved, and more urban. While this trail crosses a couple of major arterials and a few neighborhood streets, parking is generally not available at these crossings. The best access for this trail is from the northern parking lot of the Farrel-McWhirter Farm Park (see Trail 12), near the trail's eastern end. If you want to access the trail from the west, it's best to park at Sixty Acres Park on NE

116th Street—then walk 1.2 miles south on the Sammamish River Trail (see Trail 2) to the trail.

Here's a general description of the trail from east to west. From the north end of the parking lot, pick up the PSE Trail. Here the PSE heads east for 0.2 mile, paralleling the park boundary and forming the park's Perimeter Loop. Perhaps someday it will continue beyond 196th Avenue NE and connect with the Powerline Trail in the Redmond Watershed Preserve (see Trail 13).

You want to go left (west) through a pleasant forest grove. Cross Bear Creek on a bridge and then follow a dirt road, coming to busy Avondale Road NE. Use the signal to cross and then follow the trail on a much wider—and hillier—course. The way climbs and rolls along the powerline swath, passing through forest patches and brushing alongside neighborhoods. Take time to look out to the Cascades. Mount Pilchuck stands out pretty prominently.

The trail crosses 172nd Avenue NE and soon afterward follows a wider, grassier swath. It then makes a sharp bend south, a sharp bend west, and starts a long descent. After crossing NE 104th Street, the trail continues as single track. Soon come to the Redmond-Woodinville Road NE. Use caution crossing this busy roadway. The trail then steeply descends, heading into an attractive woodlot before coming to the popular paved Sammamish River Trail (see Trail 2).

If you want to continue running or hiking on the PSE Trail, look both ways for speeding bicyclists and walk a short distance right on the Sammamish River Trail. Then head left, crossing the Sammamish River on a large bridge. Turn left at a junction—then right—and follow a narrow, paved path along a small drainage creek between parking lots, a large church, and several businesses. The PSE terminates at the new paved Redmond Central Connector Trail at Willows Road. Head back the way you came, or consider the lollipop loop variation below.

GO FARTHER

Extend your run or hike by checking out the new Redmond Central Connector Trail. Follow this path left for 1.2 miles. It first parallels Willows Road—then bends east, crossing 154th Avenue NE on a bridge. Next it crosses the Sammamish River on an attractive bridge, complete with sculptures. The Redmond Central Connector continues east to downtown Redmond and connects with the Bear Creek Trail. But you want to head left (north) after the bridge on the Sammamish River Trail, returning to the PSE Trail in 1 mile.

12 Farrel-McWhirter Farm Park

DISTANCE:	More than 2 miles of trails
ELEVATION GAIN:	Up to 100 feet
HIGH POINT:	175 feet
DIFFICULTY:	Easy
FITNESS:	Runners, walkers, hikers
FAMILY-FRIENDLY:	Yes, but note some trails are open to horses
DOG-FRIENDLY:	On leash
AMENITIES:	Restrooms, water, interpretive displays, picnic tables and shelter, children's animal farm, orienteering course
CONTACT/MAPS:	City of Redmond Parks and Recreation
BEFORE YOU GO:	Park open 7:00 AM to dusk
GPS:	N 47°41.598', W 122°04.869'

GETTING THERE

Driving: From Bellevue, follow I-405 north for 1 mile. Then take the exit for State Route 520 east. After 6.3 miles, SR 520 becomes Avondale Road NE. Continue straight on Avondale Road NE for 1 mile and bear right onto NE Novelty Hill Road. Then drive 0.4 mile on NE Novelty Hill Road and turn left onto NE Redmond Road. Continue on this road for 0.5 mile and turn left into the park, proceeding a short distance to trail-head parking.

Transit: King County Metro line 224 stops on NE Novelty Hill Road.

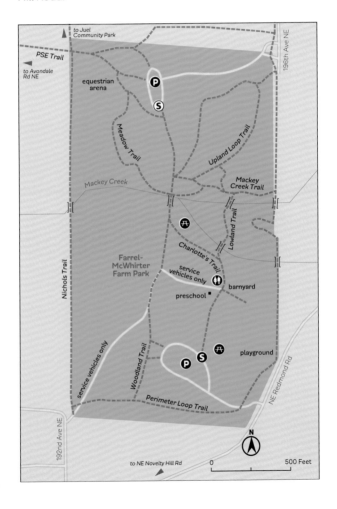

A small, family-friendly park set amid horse farms, tony sub-divisions, and remnant rural pockets, Farrel-McWhirter offers a peaceful reprieve from nearby buzzing-with-activity Redmond. Retaining much of its farm roots, this park is favored by equestrians and animal-loving children. But there are a couple of miles of quiet trails weaving through tall timber that will satisfy pedestrians. And if that's not enough, you can continue running or hiking on the PSE (Puget Sound Energy) Trail (Trail 11), which brushes through the park.

GET MOVING

This little 68-acre park is often overlooked by hikers and runners due to its proximity to the much larger Redmond Watershed Preserve (see Trail 13). That's good news if you want a peaceful stroll. Only one of the park's trails is open to bikes and there are several hiker-only paths. Start your visit by hiking north up the wide main path, soon coming to the barnyard. Here find a shelter and kiosk with all kinds of interesting historic information about the property. You're likely to see plenty of children here too, as this park with its animal farm is a popular destination for field trips.

From here the paved Charlotte's Trail skirts a pasture before entering a forest of mature firs. It crosses Mackey Creek and passes several side trails before coming to the less used northern parking area in 0.4 mile (from the south parking area). Here is an equestrian arena and more trails. The trails are all short, but you can get a decent hike by piecing them together. The Lowland Trail and Perimeter Loop Trail include quaint little bridge crossings of Mackey Creek.

Follow the Perimeter Loop Trail (which includes a portion of the PSE Trail and the heavily horse-traveled Nichols Trail) for a 1.5-mile journey around the park. Skip the Nichols Trail (which actually is outside of the park on private property with an easement) and opt for the hiker-only Woodland and

A colonnade of firs along the trail

Meadow Trails instead, and you won't have to worry about stepping in a road (or rather trail) apple.

GO FARTHER

The PSE Trail (see Trail 11) passes through the northwest corner of the park. This 4-mile trail connects to several other trails, offering many opportunities for all-day hikes or long runs. For something a little shorter, follow the PSE Trail a short distance west to a junction at the park boundary. Here the Nichols Trail (Perimeter Loop Trail) heads south and a connector trail to the Juel Community Park heads north. Take the connector for an easy 0.4 mile to Juel Community Park. Enjoy gardens and perhaps a picnic here. And if you're into disc golf, go no farther.

13 | Redmond Watershed Preserve

DISTANCE:	More than 8 miles of trails
ELEVATION GAIN:	Up to 300 feet
HIGH POINT:	580 feet
DIFFICULTY:	Easy to moderate
FITNESS:	Runners, walkers, hikers, cyclists
FAMILY-FRIENDLY:	Yes, but note trails open to mountain bikes and horses
DOG-FRIENDLY:	Prohibited
AMENITIES:	Restrooms, benches, interpretive displays, picnic tables, water
CONTACT/MAPS:	City of Redmond Parks and Recreation
GPS:	N 47°41.780', W 122°03.050'

GETTING THERE

Driving: From Bellevue, follow I-405 north for 1 mile. Then take the exit for State Route 520 east. After 6.3 miles, SR 520 becomes Avondale Road NE. Continue straight on Avondale Road NE for 1 mile and bear right onto NE Novelty Hill Road. Stay on NE Novelty Hill Road for 2.3 miles and then turn left into the Redmond Watershed Preserve. Continue a short distance for trailhead parking.

Transit: King County Metro line 224

One of the finest parks on the Eastside, the Redmond Watershed Preserve contains mature forest, rich wetlands, a deep ferny ravine, and a well-groomed trail system. It's a favorite spot for area bird watchers, trail runners, and hikers young and old. Take to one of the short nature trails or spend all day here exploring more than 8 miles of trails on 800 acres of emerald splendor.

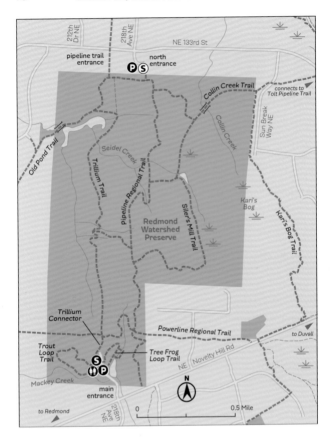

GET MOVING

The City of Redmond acquired this tract from Weyerhaeuser in the 1920s for a future water supply. But little Seidel Creek, which drains the property, didn't quite cut it for water quality. The city held on to the property and considered several industrial uses for it. Meanwhile, Weyerhaeuser developed its adjacent lands. This left the watershed parcel as a remnant large, green space in a sea of suburbia. In 1997 the property opened as a preserve, and while hiking, biking, and horse-back riding are welcomed and encouraged, the preserve has restrictions (like no dogs) to help protect resident wildlife.

The trails in the preserve are well marked and distances are given at many of the intersections. Some of the trails are hiker-only, if you don't care to share with bikes or horses. From the small picnic area near the main trailhead, find two short nature trails perfect for easy strolls with young kids. The 0.3-mile Tree Frog Loop Trail leads east to a lookout over a small pond. It's paved, making it accessible for wheelchairs. The trail leading west is the Trout Loop Trail, a pleasant, forested, 0.6-mile path near Mackey Creek.

Find the Trillium Connector at the parking lot's northern end. This wide, smooth trail acts as the portal to the core of the preserve. It soon comes to a junction with the Powerline Regional Trail at a powerline swath. The way left heads 0.5 mile to NE 112th Street. It does not connect with the PSE Trail (see Trail 11). The way right drops into a ravine and quickly climbs out, reaching a junction with the Pipeline Regional Trail at 0.3 mile. From here you can go right (south) or continue east on the Powerline Regional Trail, leaving the preserve and connecting to the extensive Redmond Ridge Trails system (see Trail 14).

The Pipeline Trail travels north for about 1.9 miles, rolling through the preserve and connecting to several trails, as well as a trailhead parking area (alternative start) off 218th Avenue NE. At the Pipeline Trail's northern reaches, you can return to the Trillium Connector Trail junction via the Trillium Trail. This 1.8-mile path drops to a small pond—then crosses several small creeks before winding out of a deep ravine cradling Seidel Creek. It is a beautiful trail through an attractive forest, with a lot of vine maples adding golden hues during the autumn months. At the small pond, a side trail leads west along the shore before leaving the preserve for private property. The complete Pipeline–Seidel Creek loop is 4.2 miles.

Hikers on the Tree Frog Loop Trail

A longer, more interesting loop involves leaving the Pipeline Trail for the Siler's Mill Trail—then taking the Collin Creek Trail back to the Pipeline Trail to the Trillium Trail. This loop is about 5 miles. There are shortcut trails if you want to shorten these loops or add a variation.

The hiker-only Siler's Mill Trail is nearly level as it follows an old logging railroad grade for much of its way. It also skirts a large wetland complex where wildlife can often be observed. In 1.4 miles it reaches the Collin Creek Trail. For the long park loop, turn left at this junction and follow the Collin Creek Trail 0.3 mile to the Pipeline Trail. If you opt to go right here, you'll cross an old drainage ditch and leave the preserve in 0.4 mile, reaching a junction. The trail leading right is the 1.3-mile Kari's

Bog Trail (part of the Redmond Ridge Trails complex). The Collin Creek Trail continues straight, connecting to the Tolt Pipeline Trail (see Trail 3) in 1 mile, near the Kathryn Taylor Equestrian Park.

GO FARTHER
Combine with the Redmond Ridge Trails (see Trail 14) or the Tolt Pipeline Trail (see Trail 3) for some serious all-day running or hiking.

14 Redmond Ridge Trails

DISTANCE:	More than 20 miles of trails
ELEVATION GAIN:	Up to 300 feet
HIGH POINT:	600 feet
DIFFICULTY:	Easy
FITNESS:	Runners, walkers, hikers, cyclists
FAMILY-FRIENDLY:	Yes, but note some trails open to mountain bikes and horses
DOG-FRIENDLY:	On leash
AMENITIES:	Restrooms at Redmond Ridge Park
CONTACT/MAPS:	Redmond Ridge Association
GPS:	N 47°41.373', W 122°02.138'

GETTING THERE
Driving: From Bellevue, follow I-405 north for 1 mile. Then take the exit for State Route 520 east. After 6.3 miles, SR 520 becomes Avondale Road NE. Continue straight on Avondale Road NE for 1 mile and bear right onto NE Novelty Hill Road. Stay on NE Novelty Hill Road for 2.8 miles and then turn right onto Redmond Ridge Drive NE. Continue for 0.3 mile and turn left onto NE Alder Crest Drive. After 0.1 mile, turn right into Redmond Ridge Park for the trailhead and parking.

Transit: King County Metro lines 224, 232 stop on NE Novelty Hill Road.

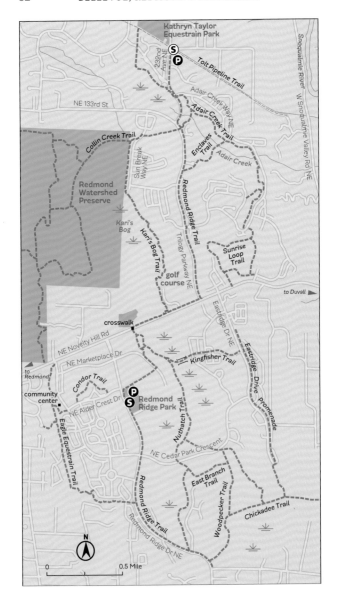

Kathryn Taylor Equestrain Park

192nd Ave NE

S
P

Tolt Pipeline Trail

Snoqualmie River

W Snoqualmie Valley Rd NE

Adair Creek Way NE

NE 133rd St

Adair Creek Trail

Collin Creek Trail

Enclaves Trail

Adair Creek

Sun Break Way NE

Redmond Watershed Preserve

Redmond Ridge Trail

Kari's Bog

Kari's Bog Trail

Trilogy Parkway NE

Sunrise Loop Trail

golf course

to Duvall

Eastridge Dr NE

crosswalk

NE Novelty Hill Rd

Kingfisher Trail

NE Marketplace Dr

Eastridge Drive Promenade

to Redmond

Condor Trail

community center

NE Alder Crest Dr

P
S

Redmond Ridge Park

Nuthatch Trail

Eagle Equestrain Trail

NE Cedar Park Crescent

East Branch Trail

Redmond Ridge Trail

Woodpecker Trail

Chickadee Trail

Redmond Ridge Dr NE

N

0   0.5 Mile

Run, walk, or hike more than 20 miles of well-marked and well-maintained trails within the planned urban village of Redmond Ridge. Lying between the subdivisions, commercial warehouses, and retail centers are large forested buffers protecting sprawling wetlands. Traversing those forests and wetlands, these trails will at times have you feeling like you're deep in the backcountry—not in a planned development.

GET MOVING

When the Redmond Ridge development was approved on Union Hill in the early 1990s, it was not without some controversy. Proceeding with this development of nearly 5000 residential units—plus business parks and an eighteen-hole golf course—required establishing a new urban growth area noncontiguous from established urban growth areas. The project went through, but fortunately nearly half of the 2100 acres of this former tree farm were retained as open space. And planners constructed an elaborate trail system to traverse the development and connect to existing regional trails. If you are looking for a place to train for your next ultra-race, or some surprisingly quiet Eastside trails to explore, check out Redmond Ridge.

Redmond Ridge is in essence two developments. North of NE Novelty Hill Road is an over-fifty-five community centered on a golf course. South of the arterial, the housing is mixed with retail and business centers. Two distinct trail systems traverse the areas, and both are well marked and well maintained. The paved Redmond Ridge Trail traverses both areas from north to south and threads them together. The best place to start your explorations of the ridge is from Redmond Ridge Park, where ample parking is available. Here you can set out on Redmond Ridge Trail and connect to a myriad of soft-surface trails for loops short and long. Below is a brief description of some of the ridge's trails.

REDMOND RIDGE TRAIL

This wide, paved King County trail primarily parallels Redmond Ridge Drive NE and Trilogy Parkway NE. It is the least interesting of the area's trails but is great for jogging strollers and allows access to many of the region's trails. It allows safe crossing (via a signal) of NE Novelty Hill Road. Don't forget to close the wildlife gates where the trail comes upon this busy arterial. The entire trail is 4.4 miles long, beginning south near NE 80th Street and ending north at the Kathryn Taylor Equestrian Park at the Tolt Pipeline Trail (see Trail 3).

NUTHATCH TRAIL

This 2.3-mile, nearly level trail is one of the ridge's most visually appealing. It travels through the heart of the southern half of the ridge, almost entirely in thick forest and along large wetland areas. Bird and wildlife observations are good. Combine it with the Redmond Ridge Trail for a 4.4-mile loop. And consider veering off on the western end of the Kingfisher Trail for a long bridged crossing of one of those big wetlands.

EAGLE EQUESTRIAN TRAIL

Despite the name, it's open to pedestrians and popular with them. This 1.4-mile path runs along a wide pipeline swath at the ridge's western boundary and connects to the community center. You can access it by walking down the Redmond Ridge Trail for 0.9 mile. Return to Redmond Ridge Park via the 0.4-mile Condor Trail, which travels up a secluded ravine and includes a short walk on sidewalks along NE Alder Crest Drive.

KARI'S BOG TRAIL

This trail north of NE Novelty Hill Road is a real treat to run or walk. It skirts the golf course and some homes, but it primarily passes through towering timber along a sprawling bog. There is an observation deck along the way. The trail can

Bridge on the Kingfisher Trail

be accessed by following the Redmond Ridge Trail 0.9 mile north from Redmond Ridge Park.

COLLIN CREEK TRAIL

Access this trail from the northern end of Kari's Bog Trail. From here you can head left to the Redmond Watershed Preserve or right through big trees on an old roadway. This trail eventually crosses the Trilogy Parkway NE and the Redmond Ridge Trail twice. It also passes by a large wetland pond. It ends in 1.1 miles at the Tolt Pipeline Trail. From Redmond Ridge Park, combine the Redmond Ridge Trail with the Kari's Bog and Collin Creek Trails for a big, 6.1-mile loop.

GO FARTHER
Combine with trails in the Redmond Watershed Preserve (see Trail 13) or the Tolt Pipeline Trail (see Trail 3) for some serious all-day running or hiking.

15 Marymoor Park

DISTANCE:	More than 5 miles of trails
ELEVATION GAIN:	Minimal
HIGH POINT:	45 feet
DIFFICULTY:	Easy
FITNESS:	Runners, walkers, hikers, cyclists
FAMILY-FRIENDLY:	Yes
DOG-FRIENDLY:	Yes, and off-leash area
AMENITIES:	Restrooms, benches, interpretive displays, picnic tables, water, playgrounds, sports fields, velodrome, historic structures
CONTACT/MAPS:	King County Parks
BEFORE YOU GO:	Parking day fee (or apply with King County Parks for multiple day permits)
GPS:	N 47°39.604', W 122°06.654'

GETTING THERE
Driving: From Bellevue, follow I-405 north for 1 mile. Take the exit for State Route 520 east and drive for 4.7 miles. Then take the W. Lake Sammamish Parkway exit and turn right onto W. Lake Sammamish Parkway NE. After 0.2 mile, turn left onto NE Marymoor Way and enter the park. Continue for 0.9 mile and turn right on a park road leading to Parking Lot G. In 0.1 mile, come to parking and the trailhead for Audubon Bird Loop.

   Transit: King County Metro line 224

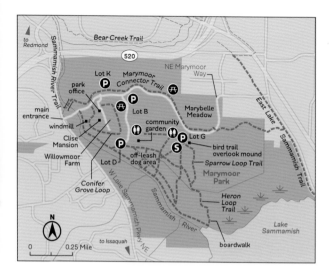

One of King County's oldest, largest, and most popular parks, Marymoor offers a wide array of recreational activities. Bicyclists love the park for its paved trails and velodrome. Hikers, runners, walkers, and especially walkers with four-legged companions flock to this sprawling 640-acre park as well. The park is a popular area for concerts and events too, so plan accordingly if you want to avoid crowds.

GET MOVING

Roughly half of this park is a natural area protecting the largest undeveloped stretch of shoreline on Lake Sammamish. Here among marshes the Sammamish River begins its journey to Lake Washington. The other half of the park is dedicated to sports fields and facilities and a historic district sporting an impressive mansion and trees.

If you seek an easy paved path, make for the Marymoor Connector Trail. This path meanders across the park from west to east for 1.5 nearly flat miles, connecting the Sammamish

Observation deck along Lake Sammamish

River Trail (see Trail 2) with the East Lake Sammamish Trail (see Trail 30). The eastern reaches are particularly attractive. Here the trail traverses a grassy wetland before entering forest. There are various paved paths that branch off this trail if you want to snoop around the park. Be sure to walk on the right, allowing cyclists to safely pass.

Area dog owners know Marymoor for its 40-acre dog park. One of the largest dog parks in the region, it allows you and your furry friend to walk or run free on trails that traverse meadows and forest and hug the Sammamish River.

The best hiking in the park is on the Audubon Bird Loop, composed of the Sparrow Loop and Heron Loop Trails. The Eastside Audubon Society helped in the development of this interpretive trail. From Parking Lot G the trail begins near an overlook mound. It then traverses a grassy meadow where a small loop can also be made. Next it crosses a small creek and enters a beautiful forest harboring healthy stands of Oregon ash. The trail then takes to a boardwalk, traveling across productive marsh and reaching a splendid viewpoint across Lake Sammamish.

The trail then heads northwest through marsh and riparian forest, following the Sammamish River. At 0.8 mile it comes to a gate and enters the off-leash area. If you do not want to be around scores of dogs running free, turn around here. Otherwise continue, soon coming to a small bridge and then a wide pathway. There are good river views and a lot of splash zones for the doggies. At 1.3 miles the trail leaves the off-leash area and reaches Parking Lot D.

Here you can continue past the community garden and across a field and return to your start in 0.4 mile. Better yet, extend your hike by adding on the 0.4-mile Conifer Grove Loop. This section of trail follows paved paths around the historic Clise Mansion, complete with its windmill. This area of the park was once the Willowmoor Farm, developed by Seattle banker James Clise in the early 1900s. Clise raised Morgan horses and Scottish Ayrshire cattle here. His grounds are graced with various ornamental heritage trees. The estate was designed by the Olmsted Brothers of New York's Central Park and Seattle's Necklace of Parks fame. The entire property is on the National Register of Historic Places. It is a delight to walk through any time of year.

GO FARTHER

For a nice urban walk or run from the park, follow the paved Sammamish River Trail north for 0.7 mile and then follow the Bear Creek Trail east for 1 mile. Walk the paved Redmond Central Connector Trail west for 1.1 miles through the heart of Redmond back to the Sammamish River Trail and follow it south 1.1 miles to return to the park.

16 Mercer Slough Nature Park

DISTANCE:	More than 7 miles of trails
ELEVATION GAIN:	Up to 75 feet
HIGH POINT:	100 feet
DIFFICULTY:	Easy
FITNESS:	Runners, walkers, hikers, cyclists
FAMILY-FRIENDLY:	Yes
DOG-FRIENDLY:	On leash
AMENITIES:	Restrooms, environmental learning center, water, benches, interpretive signs, picnic tables
CONTACT/MAPS:	City of Bellevue Parks and Community Services
GPS:	N 47°35.557', W 122°10.965'

GETTING THERE

Driving: From Bellevue, take exit 12 on I-405 and head west on SE 8th Street. Then immediately turn left onto 118th Avenue SE and proceed 0.5 mile to parking and the trailhead on your right. If lot is full, there is another parking area a short distance south.

Transit: King County Metro lines 249, 555, 556 stop at the trailhead on Bellevue Way SE.

The crown jewel of the City of Bellevue's park system, the Mercer Slough Nature Park protects 320 acres of prime wildlife habitat just minutes from downtown. The largest wetland on Lake Washington, here you can explore boggy deciduous forest, a historic blueberry farm, and a channel teeming with birds and paddlers. Boardwalks and wood-chipped trails allow for fairly dry foot passage in this wetland wonderland.

GET MOVING

This land was once a large bay on Lake Washington, but the opening of the Ship Canal in 1917 lowered the lake level

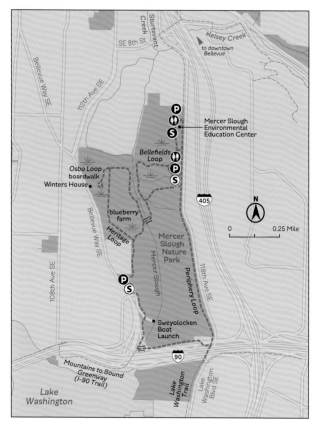

by nine feet and transformed this area into boggy, unnavigable wetland. A channel was later cut through the area, in essence creating the slough that connects Kelsey Creek to Lake Washington. The slough is now a beloved canoe trail. The Bellevue Parks Department offers guided canoe trips from May through September (contact department for details), if you want to give your feet a break and do some paddling.

The park contains a slew of history as well as wildlife. Aaron Mercer (brother of Thomas Mercer, one of Seattle's

Boardwalk near Mercer Slough

first pioneers and the man who named Lake Washington) homesteaded here in 1869. In the early twentieth century, Frederick and Cecelia Winters began a wholesale floral operation here. Their home remains and is now on the National Register of Historic Places and is open for events and rentals (but is currently closed during light rail construction). In the late 1940s, a large blueberry farm was established at the slough. Much of this farm is still in operation (leased through the parks department), and you can hike around it.

From the Mercer Slough Environmental Education Center (definitely worth checking out), follow a trail down by some wetland pools and past some mature timber. It then climbs a bit and drops off a forested bluff to connect with the Bellefields Loop Trail in about 0.3 mile. The 0.8-mile loop goes left or right, with one spur leading to additional parking, one spur leading to the paved Periphery Loop Trail, and one spur leading to the Heritage Loop Trail.

The Bellefields Loop Trail travels on boardwalks and wood chips across bogs sporting dogwoods, birches, hazelnuts, cascara, and Nootka roses. The loop also brushes along the slough in a few places, allowing for some observation of the waterway. Look for waterfowl, otters, and mink among the myriad of wildlife found here.

Take the spur along the slough from the loop and soon come to a bridged crossing of the slough. This is an even better spot to watch for wildlife—and paddlers. Just across the bridge, the trail connects to the 1-mile Heritage Loop Trail, which travels along the slough and around historic blueberry fields. Enjoy views across the blueberry bushes to skyscrapers in the background for a mixing of old Bellevue with new Bellevue.

The Osbo Loop takes off from the Heritage Loop. This trail is entirely on boardwalks, and it passes rhododendrons and an old greenhouse before ending at the historic Winters House. You probably noticed by now from trail signposts that some of the park's trails make up the Lake to Lake Trail. This is a long-distance trail (with some sidewalk sections) that connects Lake Washington with Lake Sammamish. It threads together several of the city's parks and greenbelts and traverses the city west to east. There are a couple of variations and all together it includes more than 10 miles of trail.

From the Heritage Loop, you can continue on the Lake to Lake Trail (which also includes part of the Bellefields Loop) southwest 0.2 mile to alternative parking (near the new light rail) and the paved 4.5-mile Periphery Loop Trail. You can return to your start by following this trail in either direction—but heading left (south) is far more interesting, taking you past the Sweyolocken Boat Launch where it connects to the paved Mountains to Sound Greenway (I-90 Trail).

The I-90 Trail is a favorite bike path providing access west to Mercer Island and Seattle. Watch for bikes as you follow this trail east—first on an arched bridge over the slough and then beneath freeway bridges, where you'll come to the paved Lake Washington Trail at 118th Avenue SE. Now head left on the Lake Washington Trail and return to your start in 1.1 miles.

PRESERVING A LANDSCAPE FROM MOUNTAINS TO SOUND

Stuck in traffic? Childhood favorite outdoor haunt now sprouting warehouses? Timberlands where you once hiked and hunted now covered in tract housing? It's no secret that the greater Seattle area is booming. It has been for decades—and lately the growth has been astronomical. Seattle now boasts more than 700,000 residents, King County has more than 2.2 million, and the greater Seattle metropolitan area more than 4 million. With this kind of population pressure, the very thing that attracts so many folks here—the region's natural beauty and outdoor lifestyle—is being threatened.

Recognizing this threat back in 1990, a group of citizens, led by the Issaquah Alps Trails Club, conducted a march from Snoqualmie Pass to the Seattle waterfront to bring attention to the threat of uncontrolled growth and sprawl. Under the leadership of Jim Ellis, their call to protect the region's landscapes and ways of life resulted, in 1991, in the creation of the Mountains to Sound Greenway Trust.

The Trust's mission was to establish a Mountains to Sound Greenway: a 1.5-million-acre landscape of vibrant urban centers, viable rural lands, and protected wildlands woven together along the I-90 corridor from Seattle to Ellensburg. Today they continue to work through a coalition of environmentalists, timber companies, farmers, developers, government officials, business leaders, and numerous nonprofits. The common thread among all is the desire to maintain and support healthy, vital, and livable communities. After nearly thirty years of work, more than 900,000 acres in the greenway are now publicly owned, from municipal parks to national forest lands. An additional 100,000 acres of land are conserved as private working forests.

In 2019 thanks to the Trust working with Washington's senators and local members of Congress, the greenway was declared a National Heritage Area (NHA). NHAs are designated by Congress to encourage the preservation and appreciation of historic sites. They are not federally owned but instead are administered by state governments, nonprofits, or other private corporations. And unlike national parks, NHAs are lived-in landscapes. There are more than 50 NHAs nationwide; the majority of them east of the Mississippi. The Mountains to Sound National Heritage Area is one of the first NHAs in the Pacific Northwest. For more info on the trust visit; https://mtsgreenway.org.

17 Wilburton Hill Park and Bellevue Botanical Garden

DISTANCE:	More than 3 miles of trails
ELEVATION GAIN:	Up to 150 feet
HIGH POINT:	230 feet
DIFFICULTY:	Easy
FITNESS:	Runners, walkers, hikers
FAMILY-FRIENDLY:	Yes
DOG-FRIENDLY:	Prohibited in botanical garden; on leash in the rest of the park
AMENITIES:	Restrooms, benches, interpretive signs, water, coffee house (seasonal), visitor center, sports fields
CONTACT/MAPS:	City of Bellevue Parks and Community Services
BEFORE YOU GO:	Botanical garden open dawn to dusk
GPS:	N 47°36.528', W 122°10.670'

GETTING THERE

Driving: From Bellevue, take exit 13B on I-405 southbound and head east on NE 8th Street. After 0.6 mile, turn right onto 124th Avenue NE and proceed 0.5 mile. Then either head straight for parking and trailhead at Wilburton Hill Park, or bear right onto Main Street and proceed 0.2 mile to parking and the trailhead on your left for Bellevue Botanical Garden.

From Renton, take exit 12 on I-405 northbound and turn left onto the Lake Hills Connector, which soon becomes 116th Avenue SE. After 0.2 mile, turn right onto SE 1st Street and drive 0.2 mile. Then turn right onto Main Street and continue 0.2 mile to parking and the trailhead for Bellevue Botanical Garden on your right, or continue another 0.2 mile to parking and the trailhead on your right for Wilburton Hill Park.

Transit: King County Metro line 271 stops at 116th Avenue SE, where it is a short walk via SE 1st Street and Main Street to the park.

Two parks in one, this area is packed with splendid trails, soothing landscapes, and scenic surprises. This 120-acre hilltop park was once the site of a company logging town before a big city grew up near it. Located less than a mile from downtown Bellevue, the park feels far removed from the steel-and-glass towers. It offers a far more sedate atmosphere too. Stroll, reflect, and saunter through the park's botanical garden—or hike or run carefree throughout the park on soft-surface trails traversing mature forest.

GET MOVING

First-time visitors should head straight for the Bellevue Botanical Garden, located in this wonderful park's west end (see Trail 18 for map). Stop at the visitor center, pick up a map, and then let your senses be delighted in this 30-plus-acre display of horticultural and natural beauty.

A series of wide, smooth trails ranging from 0.1 mile to 0.5 mile weave though the garden, which is actually composed of several gardens. Check out the Waterwise Garden, Rock Garden, Native Discovery Garden, Rhododendron Glen, and the Yao Garden—a Japanese garden named for Bellevue's sister city in Japan. Check out too the ground cover garden at the Shorts House, which sits on a hilltop. The house was built in the late 1940s for the Shorts, who were looking for a rural retreat—the home is now part of the park, thanks to their donation. And the rural retreat? Today you can see Bellevue's downtown skyline from the hilltop home.

Several longer trails head out from the core garden area. Walk the rolling Lost Meadow Trail and definitely head over to the Ravine Experience Trail. Young hikers will especially delight in walking this trail, which includes a 150-foot-long suspension bridge above a small ravine. You can loop around after walking the bridge and walk it again—or follow a trail leading off the hill to the Lakes Hill Connector. A third option is a trail leading to the main area of Wilburton Hill Park, near its playground and parking area.

The cross-Bellevue Lake to Lake Trail traverses the park. You can follow it 0.25 mile from the botanical garden parking lot to the park's main parking area. From here the trail winds down the hill, reaching 128th Avenue SE in 0.3 mile. A few trails branch off it northward, traversing attractive woods, leading to bordering roads, cresting the forested hilltop, and circling the park's playfields. These are much quieter than the Lake to Lake Trail and the trails within the botanical garden.

Author and son on the Ravine Experience Trail's suspension bridge

GO FARTHER

You can easily combine a visit here with the nearby Kelsey Creek Farm Park (see Trail 18). Just follow the Lake to Lake Trail east to 128th Avenue SE. From here the trail continues along SE 4th Place on road shoulder and sidewalk for 0.25 mile to the park. It's all downhill.

18 Kelsey Creek Farm Park

DISTANCE:	More than 2.5 miles of trails
ELEVATION GAIN:	Up to 200 feet
HIGH POINT:	200 feet
DIFFICULTY:	Easy
FITNESS:	Runners, walkers, hikers
FAMILY-FRIENDLY:	Yes
DOG-FRIENDLY:	Prohibited in barnyard; on leash in the rest of the park
AMENITIES:	Restrooms, benches, interpretive signs, water, playground, farm animals
CONTACT/MAPS:	City of Bellevue Parks and Community Services
BEFORE YOU GO:	Farm animals are out from 9:00 AM to 3:30 PM daily
GPS:	N 47°36.349', W 122°09.897'

GETTING THERE

Driving: From Bellevue, take exit 12 on I-405 and head east on SE 8th Street. Drive 0.3 mile and continue straight at intersection with Lake Hills Connector. Now drive east on SE 7th Place for 0.5 mile. Then turn left onto 130th Place SE and continue for 0.1 mile. Turn right into Kelsey Creek Farm Park for parking and the trailhead.

Hike, run, or walk through a beautifully preserved remnant of a Bellevue before floating bridges, shopping centers, and high-tech parks. Kelsey Creek Farm Park is one of the city's most loved parks. Aside from the historic barns and farm animals,

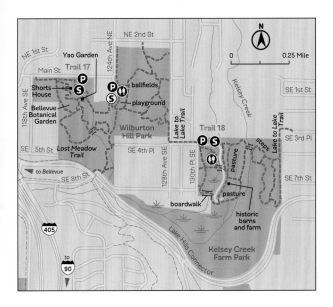

the park contains several trails that traverse wetlands, forested hillsides, and Kelsey Creek itself. The park's core sits in a small valley that feels far removed from the modern world.

GET MOVING

In the 1920s, the Duey family transformed this former stump yard (after the Hewitt-Lea Lumber Company was through with it) into the Twin Valley Dairy Farm. The park's two beautiful barns sitting atop a small ridge above surrounding pasture were built by Mr. Duey and hired hands in 1933 and 1943. Farming operations continued on the property until 1968 as suburban development crept closer. Neighbors rallied to save the 80-acre farm, and the Fisher family (who now owned it) responded by selling it to the Bellevue Parks Department for a below-market price. The new park opened in 1969 and has since been expanded to 150 acres. Today the city maintains

Stopping to check out the sheep at Kelsey Creek Farm

their parks office here and uses the farm for a wide array of educational and recreational programs.

From the parking lot, a series of trails diverges. The cross-Bellevue Lake to Lake Trail skirts the parking area. If you follow it west, it soon leaves the park to follow sidewalk and road for 0.2 mile before entering Wilburton Hill Park (see Trail 17). If you follow the trail east, it climbs up and over a small ridge, passing a couple of trails leading south. The Lake to Lake Trail then crosses Kelsey Creek on a long bridge and begins a 150-foot climb via several series of heart rate–raising steps. The trail passes four trails veering south that allow for some loop making. These side trails traverse the steep hillside, crossing several cascading creeks. Vine maples add golden touches in the fall.

The Lake to Lake Trail makes a sharp left at a powerline swath—then soon afterward makes a sharp turn right, utilizing more steps before reaching SE 3rd Place. From there the trail follows sidewalks before returning to trail and reaching the Lake to Lake Trail leading to the Lake Hills Greenbelt (see Trail 19).

The majority of visitors to Kelsey Creek Farm Park head for the farm. There's a direct paved trail making a couple of bridged creek crossings before reaching the barnyard in about 0.2 mile. Here you can follow a closed-to-traffic road and connecting trails for a 0.9-mile loop around the heart of the farm. If you're with little ones, plan on heading directly to the barnyard to admire a handful of farm animals. They're out from 9:00 AM to 3:30 PM every day of the year. Check out the historic barns and the Fraser House. The latter is one of the oldest structures in Bellevue. It was built in 1888 and was moved to the park in the 1970s.

Be sure to follow the trail that leaves the barnyard from the southwest. This trail crosses a boardwalk over flooded fields that reflect the surroundings beautifully and provide excellent wildlife habitat. The trail then passes a barn-themed playground before returning to the trailhead.

19 Lake Hills Greenbelt

DISTANCE:	3 miles of trails
ELEVATION GAIN:	Minimal
HIGH POINT:	260 feet
DIFFICULTY:	Easy
FITNESS:	Runners, walkers, hikers
FAMILY-FRIENDLY:	Yes, and jogging stroller–friendly
DOG-FRIENDLY:	On leash
AMENITIES:	Restrooms, water, benches, interpretive signs, demonstration garden, picnic shelter
CONTACT/MAPS:	City of Bellevue Parks and Community Services
GPS:	N 47°35.801', W 122°07.930'

GETTING THERE

Driving: From Bellevue, follow I-405 south to I-90 east and take exit 11B. Then follow 148th Avenue SE north for 1 mile. Next turn right onto SE 16th Street and proceed for 0.4 mile.

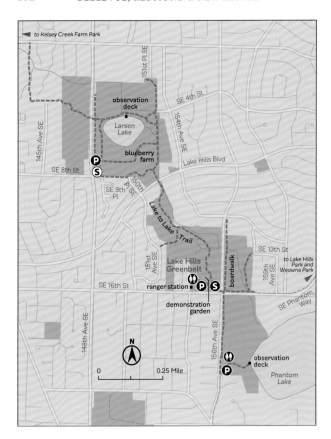

Turn left into the demonstration garden parking area and trailhead.

Transit: King County Metro line 226 stops at the greenbelt on Lake Hills Boulevard. Line 221 stops along Lake to Lake Trail on 24th Street and 168th Avenue SE.

Walk, run, or hike on well-groomed, nearly level trails through a wetland corridor between two scenic lakes. The Lake Hills

Greenbelt protects 172 acres of lakeshore, wetland meadows, forest groves, and a historic blueberry farm. The area is rife with wildlife as well as history. Much of the surrounding neighborhoods harkens back to images of a Bellevue from the 1960s, before explosive growth transformed the city into the state's fifth-largest urban center.

GET MOVING

The Lake Hills Greenbelt sits between low, rolling hills on a small plateau above Lake Washington. A rich, fertile area prized by Native peoples and Japanese immigrant farmers, suburbia encroached upon this area in the 1950s. Fortunately, conservation-minded folks were able to protect a large swath of the area between Larsen and Phantom Lakes, preserving remnant farmland and wetlands.

The greenway is traversed by the 10-mile trail network known as the Lake to Lake Trail. This trail system traverses Bellevue, connecting Lake Washington to Lake Sammamish and threading together many of the city's finest parks. The section of trail through the greenway is among the prettiest stretches of this trail.

The demonstration garden is a good place to begin your run, walk, or hike on the greenway. There is a ranger station here and a kiosk loaded with good information. There are also restrooms and parking at Phantom Lake and Larsen Lake (alternative starting areas). Pick up the trail at the east end of the garden and decide which way you want to explore first.

If you opt to go left, walk on the wide, soft-surface trail through an old peat farm. The trail is lined with willows, dogwood, and cottonwoods and is quite pretty in autumn. The way eventually traverses a grove of cedars and Sitka spruce. At 0.3 mile reach a junction. Here a trail leads left 0.1 mile to a neighborhood. The main trail continues right, passing through a meadow and coming to Lake Hills Boulevard at 0.6 mile. Carefully cross the road and enter an old blueberry farm

Winter sunset at Phantom Lake

surrounding Larsen Lake. The farm is leased and still active, so please stay on the trails. You have a lot of options here. The Lake to Lake Trail continues 0.4 mile, brushing up alongside the lakeshore (be sure to stop at the observation deck) and coming to 148th Avenue SE. The trail then continues west on its way (via trail and sidewalk) to Kelsey Creek Farm Park (see Trail 18). A side trail continues north—but better options loop around the lake. Take a longer loop of about 0.9 mile or a shorter one of about 0.75 mile. And in season, definitely stop at the farm stand southwest of the lake. Then return to your start to explore the southern end of the greenway.

Back at the demonstration garden parking area, carefully cross 156th Avenue SE and immediately come to a junction. The trail left parallels 156th Avenue SE for 0.3 mile on a boardwalk across wet meadows. The paved trail straight is part of the Lake to Lake Trail—it continues along the wet meadow for 0.1 mile to a junction. Here a spur leads left 0.2 mile back into the meadow. The Lake to Lake continues straight (see Go Farther).

Cross SE 16th Street and walk 0.2 mile to a junction. Here the Lake to Lake Trail continues straight; you want to go left 0.1 mile to an observation deck on Phantom Lake. It's a really pretty spot—peaceful too, especially in the evening—and a great place to finish your greenway exploring.

GO FARTHER

If you're looking for a nice leg stretcher, you can follow the Lake to Lake Trail for a 2.6-mile loop from Phantom Lake. On a paved path (with occasional sidewalk stretches), the trail follows alongside 156th Avenue SE, SE 24th Street, 168th Avenue SE, SE 14th Street, SE Phantom Way, and SE 16th Street. It includes one big 100-foot hill and some smaller, rolling hills. Much of the way is through quiet neighborhoods, but the trail also goes through Lake Hills Community Park (short trails) and Weowna Park (see Trail 20). And it connects to a trail leading to Robinswood Park (see Trail 21) and one leading to Spiritridge Park if you want even more exercise!

20 Weowna Park

DISTANCE:	2.5 miles of trails
ELEVATION GAIN:	Up to 500 feet
HIGH POINT:	340 feet
DIFFICULTY:	Easy to moderate
FITNESS:	Runners, hikers
FAMILY-FRIENDLY:	Yes
DOG-FRIENDLY:	On leash
AMENITIES:	Benches, interpretive signs
CONTACT/MAPS:	City of Bellevue Parks and Community Services
GPS:	N 47°35.798', W 122°06.940'

GETTING THERE

Driving: From Bellevue, follow I-405 south to I-90 east and take exit 11B. Then follow 148th Avenue SE north for 1 mile. Next turn right onto SE 16th Street (which becomes SE Phantom Way) and proceed for 1.1 miles. Turn left onto 164th Avenue SE and then immediately turn left into Lake Hills Community Park. Park here and walk the Lake to Lake Trail 0.3 mile east to Weowna Park.

Transit: King County Metro line 221

Walk through groves of big, old trees on a bluff high above Lake Sammamish. Get a good workout hiking down and up the bluff—three times if you dare. Admire lake and mountain views through gaps in the forest and marvel at an old drainage ditch that sports a small cascade in a deep ravine.

GET MOVING

Occupying a bluff above Lake Sammamish on the eastern end of Bellevue, the 90-acre Weowna Park is a key parcel in the city's Lake to Lake Greenway. It's also the eastern terminus of the 10-mile cross-Bellevue Lake to Lake Trail. While there is very limited parking (three-hour time limit) at two small trailheads at the eastern end of the park on W. Lake Sammamish Parkway SE and some street parking available on SE 16th Street, it's best to park at the Lake Hills Community Park (which also has restrooms). Then walk east on the paved Lake to Lake Trail, which parallels SE 14th Street and 168th Avenue SE. In a third of a mile, you'll reach a trailhead in Weowna Park.

You can do a short loop, a long loop, a short out-and-back, a long out-and-back, or combine them all and get a good hike and workout in this park. If you stay on the loops along the ridgetop, you won't lose or gain too much elevation. But if you decide to do any of the three trails leading to the W. Lake Sammamish Parkway, you'll get a good workout with 200 to 300 feet of climbing on each of the ascents.

The forest is old here, with many of the firs taking on old-growth characteristics. A lot of maples add golden drapes come October. Step a few feet into the forest here, and you

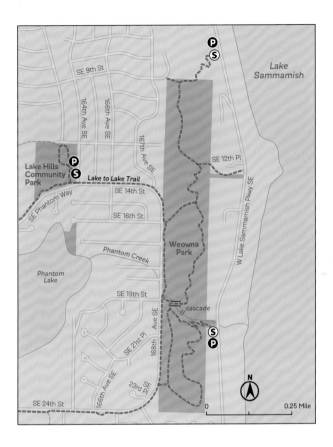

can easily forget you are surrounded by suburban develop-ments. From this trailhead, at the junction of SE 168th Avenue SE and SE 16th Street, it's 0.8 mile to the northern trailhead on W. Lake Sammamish Parkway. The trail drops to a wide ravine, where a road-trail heads right to the parkway (no parking)—then it climbs to a neighborhood trailhead at SE 9th Street. From there the trail utilizes steps and steeply drops off the bluff to reach the parkway.

Mature forest in Weowna Park

The upper loop is about 0.8 mile and is very pleasant walking, encompassing part of the paved Lake to Lake Trail. This trail crosses an old drainage ditch, which was built by an early settler in the 1890s to reverse Phantom Lake's outlet flow south to Lake Sammamish instead of flowing north to Larsen Lake and then to Lake Washington. This was done to drain the wetlands between the two lakes and open the area to cultivation. In the 1980s, the City of Bellevue restored the flow north of Phantom Lake to its original course. The lake, however, still drains south through the ditch and is now referred to as Phantom Creek. Walk over the small bridge and notice the drop to the left. Here the creek plummets over a ledge.

Beyond the bridge a trail leads along Phantom Creek, dropping down into a narrow and deep ravine where there's a small but showy cascade. This trail terminates on W. Lake Sammamish Parkway. The lower loop, which is about 0.6 mile, branches off this trail. It meanders through more old forest, offers a few glimpses through the trees, and has a little elevation gain.

21 Robinswood Park

DISTANCE:	More than 2 miles of trails
ELEVATION GAIN:	Up to 50 feet
HIGH POINT:	420 feet
DIFFICULTY:	Easy
FITNESS:	Runners, walkers
FAMILY-FRIENDLY:	Yes, and some trails jogging stroller–friendly
DOG-FRIENDLY:	On leash
AMENITIES:	Restrooms, water, benches, interpretive signs, historic structures, off-leash park, playgrounds, sports fields
CONTACT/MAPS:	City of Bellevue Parks and Community Services
GPS:	N 47°35.293', W 122°08.481'

GETTING THERE

Driving: From Bellevue, follow I-405 south to I-90 east and take exit 11B. Then follow 148th Avenue SE north for 0.7 mile. Then turn right into parking area for the park trailhead.

Transit: King County Metro lines 221, 226, 245, 271

A small park just north of office parks along busy I-405 and just east of Bellevue College, Robinswood offers a peaceful retreat. The site of a historic homestead, bustling tennis center, and sports fields, Robinswood also contains a handful of pleasant trails within its compact borders. And if these paths aren't enough to satisfy your daily step requirement, follow the adjacent Spiritridge Trail for a good little romp.

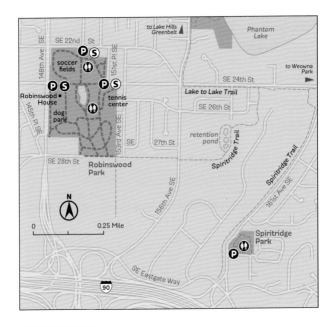

GET MOVING

Only 60 acres in size, Robinswood Park packs a lot of recreational opportunities within its borders. You'll be mostly interested in the park's trail system. But before stretching, do check
out the historic structures at the south end of the parking lot.
Here you will find three log structures making up the Miller
Homestead. The oldest was constructed by Miller in 1884—
it's one of the few original log cabins in Bellevue remaining in
good shape and in its original location. Miller then built the
log barn and the larger home now known as the Robinswood
House.

South of the homestead is a small off-leash dog park
and a series of trails taking off into the woods. The trails here
consist of a whole slew of short, interconnecting paths. They
are in good shape but unmarked, so you might get disori-
ented. No worries, though, as the park is small, and if you

come to a sidewalk or paved path (see below) just retreat to a junction and correct your turn. The forest primarily consists of second-growth Douglas firs, but it is quite stately. The terrain includes a few little dips and mounds.

After exploring the park's forest trails, check out its manicured paths. There is a perfectly level and jogging stroller–friendly, paved 0.35-mile path that loops around the soccer fields. And there is a wide, soft-surface 0.3-mile path that circles the pretty little duck pond in the heart of the park. That trail is worth doing a couple of times.

GO FARTHER

Along the park's southern border, starting from SE 28th Street between two churches, is the Spiritridge Trail. Hike or run this path, which begins paved and heads east. It passes a paved spur heading 0.3 mile to a car dealership and hotel on 156th Avenue SE.

At 0.3 mile, the Spiritridge Trail crosses 156th Avenue SE and then continues as a wide, soft-surface path onto land

Uniform forest at Robinswood Park

owned by the Boeing Company. The trail dips to a small retention pond (where another path loops around it) and then climbs a small hillside recently replanted with native vegetation. At 0.8 mile the trail connects with the Lake to Lake Trail (see Trail 19). Continue on this paved path right (east) for 0.1 mile and then continue on the Spiritridge Trail, which takes off south. The soft-surface trail continues through a forested buffer between Boeing and a quiet neighborhood along 161st Avenue SE. Despite its very suburban location, the path is quite peaceful to walk and is surrounded by greenery. The trail ends 0.6 mile from the Lake to Lake Trail (1.5 miles from Robinswood Park) at SE Eastgate Way, just beyond the small Spiritridge Park.

22 Lakemont Park

DISTANCE:	2.5 miles of trails
ELEVATION GAIN:	Up to 400 feet
HIGH POINT:	800 feet
DIFFICULTY:	Easy to moderate
FITNESS:	Runners, walkers, hikers
FAMILY-FRIENDLY:	Yes
DOG-FRIENDLY:	On leash
AMENITIES:	Restrooms, water, sports fields, picnic tables and shelters, playground
CONTACT/MAPS:	City of Bellevue Parks and Community Services; Green Trails Cougar Mountain/Squak Mountain No. 203S
GPS:	N 47°35.798', W 122°06.940'

GETTING THERE

Driving: From Bellevue, follow I-5 south to I-405 east and take exit 13. Then turn right and head south on Lakemont Boulevard SE for 1.3 miles. Next turn left onto Village Park Drive SE

Sturdy stairs in Lakemont Gorge

and after a few hundred feet turn left and proceed 0.1 mile to parking and trailhead at Lakemont Park.

Beyond the manicured grounds and storm water treatment ponds is a wilder natural park. Hike into a deep ravine among towering firs and jungle-like undergrowth and follow a tumbling, raucous Lewis Creek. Elaborate stairwells and catwalks help you negotiate the steep and rough-and-tumble landscape. Kids will love the trail fixtures while fitness junkies will embrace them for subduing calories.

GET MOVING

Up until 1990, this valley—referred to by Harvey Manning (see sidebar "Cougar Mountain's Curmudgeonly Conservationist" in the Issaquah Alps section) as the Lakemont Gorge—was a large slice of wildness above Lake Washington. I first hiked up this valley in 1989, starting at exit 13 and following survey stakes along a creek that looked like it was deep in the Cascades wilderness. However, suburbanization came and transformed hundreds of the surrounding acres

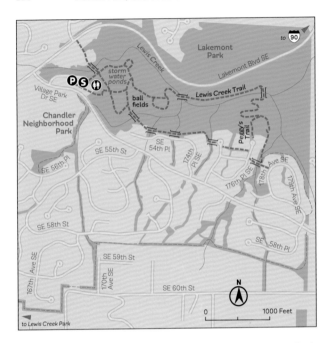

into tony housing developments. Fortunately, the ravine's most stunning section—one rife with cascades and sandstone cliffs—was preserved as a park. Some of the original primitive paths were spared too and were nicely upgraded into top-notch trails. The gorge hike is short—but it's one of the finest in Bellevue.

Several paved trails radiate from the parking area. One leads northwest, crossing Lewis Creek on a big steel bridge to a small shopping center (good place for an après-hike coffee) on Lakemont Boulevard. A couple of others loop around the storm water treatment ponds. And one leads east through several neighborhoods to 178th Avenue SE. Rack up a half mile or so walking around the ponds—then consider making one big loop by following the Lewis Creek Trail and returning via the paved trail from 178th Avenue SE.

The Lewis Creek Trail is this park's highlight, so take to this well-built, soft-surface trail. It immediately descends into the Lakemont Gorge, passing a small loop and meeting Lewis Creek at one of its many small cascades. The trail then crosses the creek and drops deeper into the emerald ravine, passing big trees and traversing steep slopes. Sturdy steel staircases and catwalks make negotiating this rough terrain manageable. Pause at the cascades. The crashing creek drowns out the noise from above and outside of the ravine, making it feel like you're deep in the wilderness.

The trail steeply drops again and then crosses the creek once more. It's now a steep climb out of the gorge on narrow tread that can be slick in wet weather. At about 0.7 mile from the trail's start, you'll reach a junction. For a shorter loop, continue straight on Peggy's Trail (which pre-1990 used to go all the way to Cougar Mountain) for 0.1 mile, coming to the paved return trail at a cul-de-sac on 176th Place SE. Then head west 0.6 mile back to your start. Stay left at the junction for a longer, more interesting return. Pass high above a tributary creek cascading into a tight ravine. Then cross that creek and at 0.25 mile come to a junction at a steel bridge. Head right on the paved trail and return to your start in 0.7 mile, or consider a longer option by heading left (see Go Farther).

GO FARTHER

From the previous junction, follow the trail left for 0.3 mile, coming to 179th Avenue SE. Turn left and cross Village Park Drive SE. Then pick up the trail again and start climbing along a greenbelt. The trail gains some decent elevation (about 400 feet) as it skirts homes and neighborhoods. There are some good views along the way out across Lake Sammamish to Mount Baker. Several side paths veer from it—just stick to the main path heading for Lewis Creek Park (see Trail 23), which you'll reach 1.4 miles from Village Park Drive SE. You can then hike north in Lewis Creek Park for 0.4 mile and take a right on a short spur to SE 56th Place. Then walk east on this road 0.2 mile to the small Chandler Neighborhood Park. From here follow a trail north 0.3 mile back to your start at Lakemont Park.

23 Lewis Creek Park

DISTANCE:	3 miles of trails
ELEVATION GAIN:	Up to 250 feet
HIGH POINT:	940 feet
DIFFICULTY:	Easy
FITNESS:	Runners, walkers, hikers
FAMILY-FRIENDLY:	Yes
DOG-FRIENDLY:	On leash
AMENITIES:	Restrooms, visitor center, water, playfields, playground, picnic shelter, benches, interpretive signs
CONTACT/MAPS:	City of Bellevue Parks and Community Services; Green Trails Cougar Mountain/Squak Mountain No. 203S
BEFORE YOU GO:	Open dawn to dusk; visitor center open Wed–Sun, 10:00 AM to 4:00 PM
GPS:	N 47°33.027', W 122°07.564'

GETTING THERE

Driving: From Bellevue, follow I-405 south to I-90 east and take exit 13. Then turn right and head south on Lakemont Boulevard SE for 2 miles. Turn left into Lewis Creek Park for parking and the trailhead.

Lewis Creek Park was established from an old farm settled by the Peltola family, who emigrated from Finland. Their former pastures and woodlots are now a wedge of wildlife-rich greenery within suburban developments. Just 55 acres, this park packs a lot in, with nearly 3 miles of trails, a visitor center, and a diverse array of habitats.

GET MOVING

Lewis Creek has its legion of loyal walkers, many of them regularly taking to the park's nearly level, half-mile loop trail. It travels through the heart of the park, traversing wetlands, former pasture, and woodlands. Birdlife is abundant, and it's not unusual to spot some larger critters as well. The trail is wide, paved in places, and includes long boardwalk sections. It's jogging stroller–friendly and welcoming to folks of all ages and abilities.

Several soft-surface trails radiate from the loop. Head off into mature forest groves and past big, old stumps shrouded in dense thickets of vine maple. Hike along Lewis Creek and to and through pocket meadows. The park is small—but if you walk, hike, or run the trails along the park's periphery, you'll

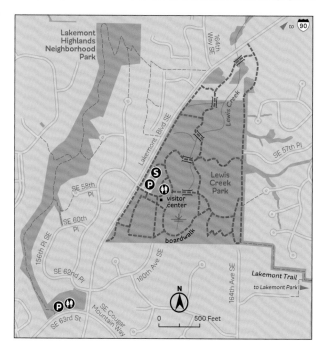

Loop trail through a small meadow

tally up 1.5 miles. Add the connecting trails for more loop options, and you can easily double your mileage. And if you're looking for harder and longer workouts, there are a couple of trails that head out of the park, giving you that opportunity (see Go Farther).

Be sure to check out the visitor center—especially if this is your first time to the park. Bellevue Parks and Community Services regularly conducts ranger-led hikes and interpretive programs here, as well as hosting programs from various conservation organizations.

GO FARTHER
Follow the Lakemont Trail out of the park to Lakemont Park (see Trail 22) and then return via a trail to the Chandler Neighborhood Park and a short road walk, for a big loop hike of 3 to 3.5 miles. You can also take a trail out of the park to where 164th Way SE meets Lakemont Boulevard SE.

Use crosswalks to cross these busy arterials, and pick up a trail through the Lakemont Highlands Neighborhood Park, a greenbelt several hundred feet above Lewis Creek. Get in a good climb and reach the south end of the park and SE 63rd Street (restroom available) in 1.4 miles. You can then carefully walk back on Lakemont Boulevard (no sidewalk; use the shoulder with caution) for about 0.25 mile before picking up a trail in Lewis Creek Park and returning to the parking lot.

24   May Creek Trail

DISTANCE:	Up to 5.9 miles roundtrip
ELEVATION GAIN:	450 feet
HIGH POINT:	400 feet
DIFFICULTY:	Moderate
FITNESS:	Runners, hikers
FAMILY-FRIENDLY:	Yes
DOG-FRIENDLY:	On leash
AMENITIES:	Restrooms, picnic tables, fuchsia garden, playground at Lake Boren; interpretive signs
CONTACT/MAPS:	City of Newcastle; Green Trails Cougar Mountain/ Squak Mountain No. 203S
GPS:	N 47°31.707', W 122°09.945'

GETTING THERE

Driving: From Bellevue, follow I-405 south and take exit 10. Turn left onto Coal Creek Parkway SE and continue south for 3.2 miles. Then turn right onto SE 84th Way and proceed for 0.1 mile. Turn right into Lake Boren Park for parking.

From Renton, follow I-405 north to exit 5. Turn right and drive State Route 900 (NE Park Drive, which becomes NE Sunset Boulevard) for 2.3 miles. Turn left onto Duvall Avenue NE (which becomes the Coal Creek Parkway SE) for 1.7 miles. Then turn left onto SE 84th Way and proceed for 0.1 mile. Turn right into Lake Boren Park for parking.

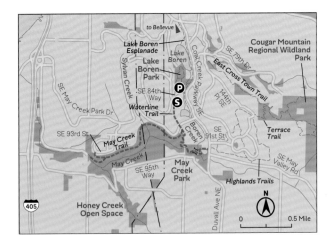

Hike along the rim of a ravine cradling May Creek via an old railroad grade. And hike into that ravine along the tumbling creek. Admire big trees and reflect at the site of a long-gone trestle—once the longest wooded railroad trestle west of the Mississippi River. This wonderful trail traverses a greenbelt park rife with scenic, natural, and historic surprises.

GET MOVING

Once a rough-and-tumble coal mining settlement that helped fuel Seattle's early development, today Newcastle is a well-to-do suburb. Place-names (Newcastle itself is named after the UK coal town Newcastle upon Tyne) and relics hidden in greenbelts scattered throughout the community attest to Newcastle's industrial past. This trail, along with the one along Coal Creek (see Trail 25), offers great historical jaunts—and some pretty scenery too.

Lake Boren Park, with its ample parking and restrooms, is the logical spot to access the May Creek Trail. From the park, walk west along SE 84th Way for a short distance, coming to the Waterline Trail. Turn left here and follow this path for 0.6

mile to SE May Creek Park Drive (limited parking). Cross the road and come to the May Creek Trail. A good portion of this path utilizes an old railroad line. Old Newcastle had a viable timber industry, as well as a coal mining industry, and this line was used to transport both.

You can go left or right here. My suggestion—go both ways (one before the other, of course). The way right heads west, immediately following part of the original rail bed. Admire old cuts and look for original stonework along the way. The trail travels along the edge of a ravine, cradling cascading May Creek. Towering cottonwoods line the way. At 0.5 mile from SE May Creek Park Drive, cross Sylvan Creek and come to an orchard near a local trail access point.

The trail continues 0.7 mile west high above May Creek, coming to an unmarked junction near an interpretive site. Here two 1200-foot-long, 238-feet-high trestles (one narrow gauge, the other standard) spanned the creek and ravine from 1878 until 1933. They were at one time among the largest wooden structures west of the Mississippi River. From this spot, the trail continues up steps to terminate in 0.1 mile in a residential area (no parking). The trail from the unmarked junction drops into the ravine, reaching May Creek in about 0.25 mile. Local trail advocates hope to someday continue this trail across the creek to parklands in abutting Renton.

Retrace your steps back to the junction at SE May Creek Park Drive and then explore the eastern stretch of this trail. Departing from the rail bed, the path passes an old mail truck resting in the woods before switchbacking down into the ravine. The way then travels right along May Creek before slowly climbing back out of the ravine. It crosses Boren Creek on a sturdy bridge—then continues winding out of the ravine, coming to a short paved section before terminating at 0.8 mile on Coal Creek Parkway SE. You can walk on sidewalk a short distance right to the bridge spanning the creek and peer down for a good look before heading back to the trailhead.

SEATTLE'S HISTORIC CARBON FOOTPRINT

Seattle was not founded on software, coffee, aerospace, or e-commerce. The city's initial economic boom was due to coal mining. Most folks equate this carbon-based energy source with Appalachia, Illinois, and the Powder River Basin—not the Pacific Northwest. However, from 1863 to 1963, more than eleven million tons of coal were extracted from mines in Newcastle, Washington.

The county's first major industry, coal mining was financed by investors from California and the East Coast. In the 1860s, coal extracted from Newcastle and the nearby town of Coal Creek helped propel the newly incorporated city of Seattle from a small backwater to a major port city just twenty years later. The coal was initially barged from the Eastside to Seattle for export before railroads were built in the 1870s.

Coal mining was (and still is) arduous and dangerous work. Companies heavily relied on immigrant labor. The communities around Newcastle were diverse places, home to folks from China, Wales, Scotland, Italy, Finland, France, Ireland, Belgium, England, and Sweden, as well as African Americans who migrated from southern states. Coal production peaked during World War I. Afterward, labor strife, the Great Depression, and the use of oil for energy greatly diminished demand. Eventually, timber production surpassed coal mining in the hills east of Seattle.

The old Newcastle and the company towns of Coal Creek, Red Town, Rainbow Town, and others are gone. However, relics exist attesting to their place in history. Walk around Cougar Mountain looking for them. Walk down the Red Town Trail, which used to be Hill Street in a town that contained more than fifty homes, a church, hotel, saloon, and school. The nearby Ford Slope (whose mine shaft you can still see) was Newcastle's biggest producer of coal. And while much of the surroundings today sports maturing forests, note that the landscape was greatly altered during the mining days. Hills were leveled for strip mines and other hills created out of mining debris and tailings. Many of the creeks also follow courses altered during the mining days.

GO FARTHER

For a big loop and adventure, carefully cross Coal Creek Parkway at a crosswalk near the entrance of the Highlands development (just north of the May Creek Trail terminus) and then follow a trail along the southern or northern periphery of the Highlands for 1.1 miles, coming to a trailhead for the Terrace Trail on 144th Place SE (limited parking).

Then take this beautifully constructed trail, climbing through tall timber and boulders up a steep ridge. At 0.6 mile it comes to a junction high on a ridge at the edge of Newcastle Hills neighborhoods. You can continue right, climbing even higher and passing a viewpoint before entering the Cougar Mountain Regional Wildland Park and eventually coming to the De Leo Wall Trail (see Trail 35) at 0.4 mile. The trail left is part of the East Cross Town Trail. Follow this fairly new trail along the ridge, gently descending and coming to SE 79th Drive in 1.1 miles. Then follow this road left 0.1 mile to a crosswalk across the Coal Creek Parkway. Here head left 0.2 mile on the 0.7-mile-long paved Lake Boren Esplanade to a paved path leading right—follow it back to your vehicle in Lake Boren Park. Still want to walk some more? Enjoy the 0.6-mile paved path in Lake Boren Park to a dock on the pretty lake.

Old mail truck along the May Creek Trail

25 Coal Creek Natural Area

DISTANCE:	5.5 miles of trails
ELEVATION GAIN:	Up to 700 feet
HIGH POINT:	650 feet
DIFFICULTY:	Easy to moderate
FITNESS:	Runners, hikers
FAMILY-FRIENDLY:	Yes
DOG-FRIENDLY:	On leash
AMENITIES:	Interpretive signs; privies at Red Town Trailhead
CONTACT/MAPS:	City of Bellevue Parks and Community Services; Green Trails Cougar Mountain/Squak Mountain No. 203S
GPS:	N 47°33.109', W 122°09.996'

GETTING THERE

Driving: From Bellevue, follow I-405 south and take exit 10. Then turn left onto Coal Creek Parkway SE and continue south for 1.5 miles. Just before a bridge over Coal Creek, turn left into Red Cedar Trailhead parking area.

A **445-acre greenbelt wedged between** Bellevue and New-castle, the Coal Creek Natural Area protects important wildlife habitat, preserves historic relics, and offers excep-tional hiking and trail running opportunities. Travel through an emerald ravine that once housed a flurry of industrial activity. Look for coal mining and railroad relics among capti-vating cascades and towering timber.

GET MOVING

The trail system within the Coal Creek Natural Area can be accessed from several trailheads. The Red Cedar Trailhead off Coal Creek Parkway is the preferred start for heading up and then back down the upper reaches of the natural area. Unfortunately, the parking lot is small and rapidly fills on weekends. Consider parking at the trail's eastern terminus at the Red Town Trailhead in Cougar Mountain Regional Park—or the YMCA or new Cinder Mine Trailheads, both located off of Newcastle Golf Club Road.

Most visitors immediately begin hiking or running east (upstream). However, you can also head west (downstream) on a section of trail far less traveled. The downstream portion ducks under the Coal Creek Parkway and soon comes to a junction. The trail left leads 0.6 mile to SE 60th Street. The Coal Creek Trail continues right, soon passing a spur leading right to Coal Creek Parkway.

The trail then climbs above the creek, traverses steep slopes, and travels along a rib above Coal Creek and a tributary. It then descends, crosses the tributary, and at 1.2 miles from the Red Cedar Trailhead comes to a junction with a short spur leading left to 121st Avenue SE. The main way then crosses another tributary and ends in 0.2 mile at a staircase leading up to 119th Avenue SE. There is no parking here—but you can park at the Newcastle Beach Park and follow the paved Lake Washington Trail 0.5 mile north. Then walk 0.2

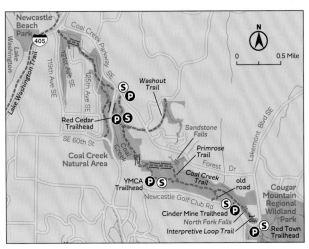

Mossy overhanging limbs along the Coal Creek Trail

mile east on bike path and sidewalk, darting under I-405 to reach the trail.

Heading east (upstream) from the Red Cedar Trailhead has you on a well-worn section of trail traveling right along the cascading creek. The way passes two trails leading left— one heads 0.3 mile to Forest Drive (alternative start); the other is the Washout Trail, leading to a greenbelt beyond Forest Drive. The trail continues up a deep, lush, emerald ravine. Housing developments cover the surrounding hillsides, but they're out of view from below, giving the trail a feeling of being much wilder.

The trail makes a bridged crossing of Coal Creek before coming to a junction with the Primrose Trail at 1 mile. The Coal Creek Trail continues right, climbing above the creek and reaching a 0.1-mile spur to the YMCA Trailhead before heading west on an old rail grade. It meets back up with the Primrose Trail in 0.5 mile.

The Primrose Trail offers a far more interesting route. It continues in the ravine, making a bridged crossing of the creek and traversing mossy maple groves. It then passes Sandstone Falls, a small, seasonal fanned waterfall created by storm water drainage. It then crosses the creek on a massive bridge and begins a steep ascent via steps out of the ravine bottom to reconnect with the Coal Creek Trail. En route it passes the remains of a coal cart.

The Coal Creek Trail now continues on an old railroad grade above the creek. It passes the old cinder mine near an old road and then comes to the site of an old train turntable, once used to turn trains 180 degrees in the narrow ravine. Here and farther along, interpretive signs grace the way.

The way passes a spur leading right to the new Cinder Mine Trailhead. It then comes to an old mill and flume site and pretty little North Fork Falls, feeding Coal Creek. The trail then reaches a short Interpretive Loop Trail and a deep mine air shaft before crossing the creek one more time. At 2.7 miles from the Red Cedar Trailhead, it reaches its terminus at Lakemont Boulevard SE across from the Red Town Trailhead.

GO FARTHER

You can return to the YMCA Trailhead via a 1.4-mile trail that parallels the Newcastle Golf Club Road. You can also combine this trail network with the extensive one at Cougar Mountain—and hike and run until your heart's content.

Next page: *Madronas and firs lining the trail at Luther Burbank Park (Trail 26)*

MERCER ISLAND

The largest island in Lake Washington, Mercer Island was once used as a hunting, fishing, and berry-gathering ground by members of the Mercer Family, one of Seattle's pioneer families. In the late 1800s, it became a retreat for some of Seattle's most prominent citizens as well as for some dignitaries from back east. The island was eventually connected to the Eastside by bridge in 1928 and to Seattle by a floating bridge (second longest in the world) in 1940. The latter literally paved the way for this rural island's transformation from a small community known as East Seattle into a large city suburb. In 1960 it was incorporated as the city of Mercer Island, and today this affluent community counts more than 26,000 residents. Shaped like a foot, there are several places you can set your feet in motion on trails here, including a few places where you can get a taste (albeit a small one) of Mercer Island's pre-suburban past.

26 Luther Burbank Park

DISTANCE:	More than 2 miles of trails
ELEVATION GAIN:	Up to 75 feet
HIGH POINT:	75 feet
DIFFICULTY:	Easy
FITNESS:	Runners, walkers
FAMILY-FRIENDLY:	Yes, jogging stroller–friendly and ADA-accessible trails too
DOG-FRIENDLY:	On-leash and off-leash areas
AMENITIES:	Restrooms, water, benches, interpretive signs, picnic tables, playground, beach, tennis courts
CONTACT/MAPS:	City of Mercer Island Parks and Recreation
GPS:	N 47°35.493', W 122°13.570'

GETTING THERE

Driving: From Bellevue, follow I-90 west and take exit 7 on Mercer Island. Then turn right onto SE 26th Street and proceed for 0.1 mile. Next turn left onto 84th Avenue SE and drive 0.3 mile to the trailhead at the north lot (additional parking in the south lot, also on 84th Avenue SE).

From Seattle, follow I-90 east and take exit 7A on Mercer Island. Then turn left onto 77th Avenue SE and immediately turn right onto N. Mercer Way. Continue 0.2 mile and turn left onto 81st Avenue SE. After 0.1 mile, turn right onto SE 24th Street. Drive 0.2 mile and turn left onto 84th Avenue SE. Then drive 0.2 mile to the trailhead at the north lot (additional parking in the south lot, also on 84th Avenue SE).

Transit: King County Metro line 894 stops near south lot. King County Metro lines 201, 204, 216, 550, 554, 630, 892, 981, 989 stop at N. Mercer Way and 80th Avenue SE; it's a short 0.3-mile walk to the park.

Walk or run along rippling Lake Washington shoreline and across manicured lawns lined with stately trees. This beautiful

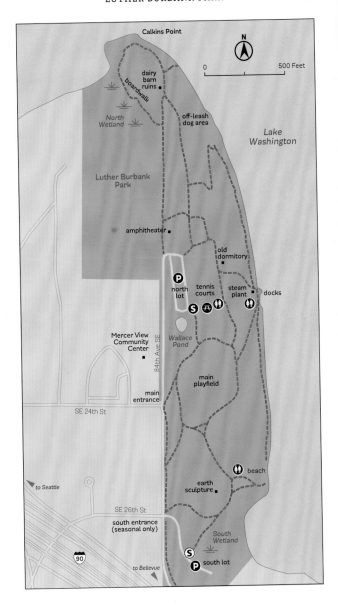

Fields and Lake Washington views at Luther Burbank Park

park on the northern tip of Mercer Island flush with joyful families, dogs and their humans, and folks of all backgrounds was once the site of a parental school for delinquent youths.

GET MOVING
Luther Burbank is a beloved 77-acre park with 0.75 mile of shoreline on Lake Washington, rolling meadows, hidden marsh, and sublime views of shimmering skyscrapers and snow-shrouded summits across sparkling waters. The park is adorned too with majestic oaks, showy madronas, and white birches, whose leaves turn golden yellow come October.

Scattered throughout the park's grounds are also restored buildings and remnant ruins of the reform school that operated here from 1904 until 1966. The school included a dairy farm, other farm operations, and gardens that the students worked in after taking classes. The predominantly urban students took well to the horticultural programs here. And to inspire them, the school's name was changed in 1931 to honor the renowned botanist Luther Burbank.

The north parking lot and trailhead provides quick access to an attractive brick building, once the school's dormitory, now housing the parks department's administration. A path behind it drops to the lakeshore, where the steam plant still stands next to an extended dock. Bustling with boats in the summer, the dock is empty during the winter and makes for a nice walk out over the lake.

Paved paths lead south from the administration building to a playground, picnic ground, and two meadows. Loop around the meadows and walk or run past an earth sculpture to the park's swim area. If it's summer, go for a dip.

Paved and soft-surface paths lead north from the administration building to fishing spots along the lake, dairy barn ruins, a wetland, a large and popular off-leash area (complete with a beach), and Calkins Point. The latter once housed a grand hotel that gained attention in 1891 when President Benjamin Harrison stayed there. Nothing remains of the hotel, but the lake views that the president enjoyed are still there—of course slightly altered, as lakeshore homes and Seattle's skyscrapers can now be seen.

Just to the south of Calkins Point is a short boardwalk nature trail that traverses the North Wetland, conjuring up scenes that perhaps the president would have been more familiar with. It's a great trail for birdwatching and escaping the commotion of the park.

27 Mercerdale Park

DISTANCE:	About 1.5 miles of trails
ELEVATION GAIN:	Up to 350 feet
HIGH POINT	280 feet
DIFFICULTY:	Easy to moderate
FITNESS:	Walkers, runners
FAMILY-FRIENDLY:	Yes
DOG-FRIENDLY:	On leash
AMENITIES:	Restrooms, water, benches, picnic tables, playground
CONTACT/MAPS:	City of Mercer Island Parks and Recreation
GPS:	N 47°34.912', W 122°14.099'

GETTING THERE

Driving: From Bellevue, follow I-90 west and take exit 7 on Mercer Island. Turn left onto Island Crest Way. Cross the freeway and immediately turn right onto SE 27th Street. Then immediately turn left onto 80th Avenue SE. Continue 0.4 mile and turn right onto SE 32nd Street. Park on street (more parking on SE 34th Street). The trailhead is located at the junction of SE 32nd Street and 77th Avenue SE.

From Seattle, follow I-90 east and take exit 7A on Mercer Island. Then turn right onto 77th Avenue SE and drive 0.4 mile to junction with SE 32nd Street. Find street parking (more

Stairway up First Hill

parking on SE 34th Street). The trailhead is located at the junction of SE 32nd Street and 77th Avenue SE.

Transit: King County Metro lines 891, 892

Looking for a great workout? Interested in an excellent fitness challenge? Then take to the more than three hundred steps that ascend from the park to First Hill. Then run or walk a series of trails traversing the hill and tally another one hundred-plus steps. And if that's not enough—there's a quarter-mile paved loop in the park perfect for sprints.

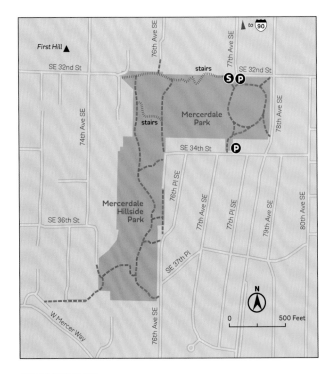

GET MOVING

Located within the commercial district of the island, little 12-acre Mercerdale Park sees its fair share of after-work walkers. The park hosts summer music festivals and a lot of other family-friendly events throughout the year. It's a park where you literally go stepping out. To many a Mercer Islander, Mercerdale means a stair workout. Leading west from the park is a wide, curving-in-places set of steps that climbs nearly 200 feet up First Hill in the adjacent 19-acre Mercerdale Hillside Park.

The steps contain a railing that runs up it slightly off-center, in essence creating two lanes. As you elevate your heart rate tackling it, the increased elevation allows for some nice viewing. Pause to catch your breath and look out at the nearby Bellevue skyline and a backdrop of Cascade peaks.

A couple of short spurs lead north to neighborhoods, and a couple of longer trails (the longest about 0.5 mile) lead south. Definitely take to these and the short trails leading off of them to residential neighborhoods. The main trail (upper one) traverses the hillside and includes some ups and downs. It also includes—as do all of the radiating trails—more steps. Big cottonwoods, cedars, and firs line the way, creating a green swath between neighborhoods above and below. However, the buzz of vehicles on I-90 and the sound of folks out and about in the distance remind you that the city is not very far away at all.

GO FARTHER

Just a few blocks north of Mercerdale Park is Aubrey Davis Park. Formerly known as the Park on the Lid, this swath of lawns and playfields was constructed on a lid over I-90. The park is named for the former mayor who fought hard to make sure that the widening of the freeway wouldn't degrade the island and diminish its residents' quality of life. The result: a series of lids over the freeway, landscaped with inviting family-friendly parks.

The paved I-90 Trail traverses the park, and you may want to run out on it to the Homer M. Hadley Memorial Bridge on Lake Washington, one of two floating bridges connecting Mercer Island with Seattle. Do be aware of cruising cyclists and the deafening noise of speeding vehicles. There are short loops and quieter trails in the park, however, where you can enjoy lake, mountain, and Seattle skyline views without the freeway commotion—the whole reason for the establishment of this park in the first place.

28 Pioneer Park

DISTANCE:	7 miles of trails
ELEVATION GAIN:	Up to 225 feet
HIGH POINT:	350 feet
DIFFICULTY:	Easy to moderate
FITNESS:	Walkers, runners, hikers
FAMILY-FRIENDLY:	Yes, some trails stroller and wheelchair accessible
DOG-FRIENDLY:	On-leash and off-leash areas
AMENITIES:	Privies
CONTACT/MAPS:	City of Mercer Island Parks and Recreation
GPS:	N 47°32.519', W 122°13.185'

GETTING THERE

Driving: From Bellevue, follow I-90 west and take exit 7 on Mercer Island. Then turn left onto Island Crest Way and proceed 3 miles. Turn left onto SE 68th Street and continue a short distance to a parking area on your left. Additional street

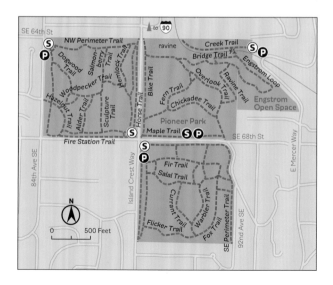

parking can be found along 84th Avenue SE (north of the junction with SE 68th Street).

From Seattle, follow I-90 east and take exit 7B on Mercer Island. Then follow Island Crest Way for 3 miles. Turn left onto SE 68th Street and continue a short distance to the parking area on your left. Additional street parking can be found along 84th Avenue SE (north of the junction with SE 68th Street).

Transit: King County Metro lines 204, 894

Hike, walk, or run through Mercer Island's largest greenbelt and experience a Mercer Island before floating bridges propelled it into suburbia. Threatened with being turned into a golf course over the years, this park has been kept in a natural state through the efforts of concerned citizens who fought to preserve it. Pioneer Park and the adjacent Engstrom Open Space's mature forests and deep emerald ravine offer serenity and a touch of wild on the island.

GET MOVING

Pioneer Park consists of three quarter-mile squared sections (quadrants), separated by roads. Add the Engstrom Open Space tract to the mix, and you have more than 120 acres of greenery to explore. Seven miles of well-developed trails traverse it all, giving you plenty of opportunity to roam. While the trails are named, most are not marked—so download a map to take along for your first couple of visits.

The busiest of the three sections is the northwest quadrant. It is also the most level. Stick to the wide NW Perimeter Trail on the quadrant's perimeter for an easy 1-mile loop. Several trails branch off for the interior. There are a few interpretive signs interspersed along these trails. Dogs can go sans leash on this section, as long as they are under strict voice control. They can also go off leash in the southeast quadrant (keep them away from horses) but must be on leash in the northeast quadrant.

Peaceful forest on Mercer Island

The southeast quadrant is the quietest of the three. All of that quadrant's trails are open to horses (only a couple trails in the northwest quadrant allow horses), but they are also open to pedestrians. It's possible to roam these trails and have them for yourself. This quadrant gently slopes to the west, allowing for a little elevation gain and loss on your loop and interior trail amblings.

The northeast quadrant, with the adjoining Engstrom Open Space tract, is the most interesting and varied part of the park—with trails leading down into a deep, creek-cradling ravine. You can cross the creek on a big bridge, following a trail to a trailhead (limited parking) on E. Mercer Way. And you can get some good elevation gain and loss on the Ravine Trail and Engstrom Loop. There are some impressive trees on this tract. And there is less invasive ivy too, which unfortunately has choked a good portion of the natural vegetation in this park. The northeast quadrant also contains a short, paved trail that parallels Island Crest Way.

GO FARTHER

Walk north on a soft-surface path paralleling Island Crest Way to Island Crest Park. West of the ballfields, find a series of well-built trails traversing the park's woods. The trails are not signed, but they're short—so you won't get lost. The old suspension bridge is gone, so loop options here are lacking (unless you utilize some of the adjacent neighborhood roads). Hike each trail out and back and enjoy the mature forest, seasonal creek, and large ravine. If you have little ones, plan on visiting Deane's Children's Park, also known as the Dragon Park.

Next page: *Beaver Lake Preserve (Trail 33)*

ISSAQUAH & SAMMAMISH

Once a small logging and farming community, today Issaquah (population 40,000) is a booming retail and residential center. Neighboring Sammamish (population 70,000) is also seeing rapid change. Both of these cities owe their explosive growth and pricey real estate to Seattle's and the Eastside's burgeoning aerospace and technology economies. These two communities, located between Lake Sammamish (one of the largest lakes in the state) and the Issaquah Alps, are highly desirable locations offering a large array of outdoor amenities, especially trails. Issaquah is one of Washington's premier trail towns, sitting at the base of the Issaquah Alps—a patchwork of public lands crisscrossed by hundreds of miles of trails. Many folks living in these communities can head right out their back door and be on a trail.

29 Lake Sammamish State Park

DISTANCE:	More than 5 miles of trails
ELEVATION GAIN:	Minimal
HIGH POINT:	40 feet
DIFFICULTY:	Easy
FITNESS:	Walkers, runners, hikers
FAMILY-FRIENDLY:	Yes, some trails stroller accessible
DOG-FRIENDLY:	On leash
AMENITIES:	Restrooms, water, picnic tables and shelter, sports fields, beach
CONTACT/MAPS:	Washington State Parks
BEFORE YOU GO:	Discover Pass required; park open 6:30 AM to dusk
GPS:	N 47°33.528', W 122°03.760'

GETTING THERE

Driving: From Bellevue, follow I-90 east and take exit 15. Then turn left onto 17th Avenue NW and proceed for 0.2 mile. Turn left onto NW Sammamish Road and continue for 0.4 mile. Turn right onto park road, enter Lake Sammamish State Park, and drive 0.4 mile to large parking area and trailhead.

Transit: King County Metro lines 217, 269, 271

Once the site of a couple of large dairy farms, today Lake Sammamish State Park is one of the few large, undeveloped areas remaining on Lake Sammamish. While this park contains ballfields and a popular beach—it also consists of a large natural area traversed by quiet trails. Walk along Issaquah Creek to old pastures and stare out at Tiger Mountain. It's a view from back in time, when Issaquah was still quite rural.

GET MOVING

To many Eastsiders, Lake Sammamish State Park is synonymous with beach. The park's wide, sandy beaches teem with

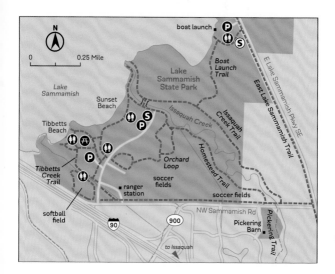

swimmers and bathers during the warmer months. During the cooler months, however, the park's beaches invite quiet wandering. But if you're looking for a long walk or good run, take to the park's trails. More than 5 miles of trails of varying surfaces—paved, dirt, and boardwalk—weave through the 500-plus-acre park. And all of them are virtually level.

A couple of paths loop near the sports fields in the southern part of the park. But the trails east of the large parking area are far more interesting. Definitely take the boardwalk trail along the west bank of Issaquah Creek to the lake. This path—complete with interpretive panels—travels across rich habitat that was once degraded by human impact. In this restored area, look for a variety of aquatic, avian, and furry inhabitants.

Back at the parking area, head east on a wide path to a bridge over Issaquah Creek. Then follow the creek upstream along the edge of a meadow—once part of a dairy farm dating back to the late 1800s. It's hard to imagine that when this park was established here in the early 1950s, Issaquah was a rural

Trail along Issaquah Creek

and quiet community. The park is now nearly surrounded by busy arterials, commercial centers, and housing.

The 1.2-mile Issaquah Creek Trail continues south, leaving the park and coming to NW Sammamish Road. You can turn right and return to the main area of the park on a paved trail. The 0.4-mile Boat Launch Trail—one of the nicest in the park— leaves the Issaquah Creek Trail midway and winds through a wet meadow to the park's boat ramp at the park's eastern end (alternative parking and start). Along this trail, look south across fields to Tiger Mountain. Vegetation along the field's edges blocks any evidence of the busy modern Issaquah, allowing your mind to wander back in time. From the boat launch area, you can also access the East Lake Sammamish Trail (see Trail 30).

Another trail, the Homestead Trail (prone to flooding), travels 0.6 mile along Issaquah Creek's western bank to the paved trail along NW Sammamish Road. Branching off this trail is the short Orchard Loop Trail, traversing yet another remnant of the park's farming heritage.

GO FARTHER

From the paved path along NW Sammamish Road, you can pick up the paved Pickering Trail. It darts under the busy road near Issaquah Creek and then meanders along the creek, passing the Pickering Barn. It then darts under the new SE 62nd Street extension and crosses Issaquah Creek. In 0.7 mile, it terminates at the East Lake Sammamish Trail. You can follow that trail north for 0.5 mile—then walk west on sidewalk along NW Sammamish Road for 0.2 mile for a loop.

30 East Lake Sammamish Trail

DISTANCE:	10.4 miles one-way
ELEVATION GAIN:	Minimal
HIGH POINT:	60 feet
DIFFICULTY:	Easy
FITNESS:	Walkers, runners, cyclists
FAMILY-FRIENDLY:	Yes, and jogging stroller–friendly
DOG-FRIENDLY:	On leash
AMENITIES:	Benches, water, interpretive signs; restrooms at Sammamish Landing and Confluence Parks
CONTACT/MAPS:	King County Parks
GPS:	N 47°40.032', W 122°06.250'

GETTING THERE

Driving: The trail can be accessed from several areas: *Northern Terminus Trailhead (Redmond):* From Bellevue, follow I-405

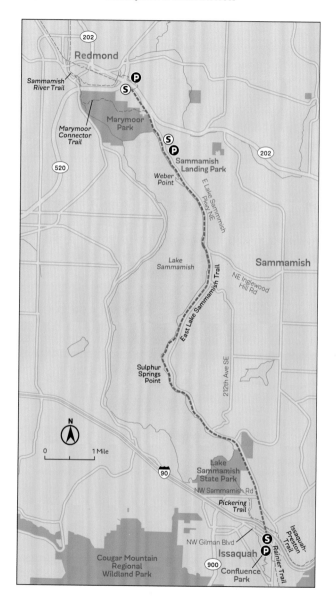

north for 1 mile. Then take the exit for State Route 520 east and drive for 5.9 miles. Take the exit for SR 202 (Redmond Way) and head east (right). Continue for 0.3 mile and then turn right onto NE 70th Street. Drive 0.1 mile, cross the trail, and turn left to the parking area paralleling trail. *Sammamish Landing Park (Sammamish):* From Bellevue, follow I-405 north for 1 mile. Then take the exit for SR 520 east and follow it for 5.9 miles. Take the exit for SR 202 (Redmond Way) and head east (right). Continue for 0.5 mile and bear right onto E. Lake Sammamish Parkway NE. Drive for 1.3 miles to parking on your left. *Southern Terminus near Confluence Park (Issaquah):* From Bellevue, follow I-405 south to I-90 and then head east, taking exit 17 in Issaquah. Turn right (south) onto Front Street and proceed for 0.3 mile, making a sharp right turn onto Rainier Avenue. Proceed 0.1 mile to parking on your left at Confluence Park.

Transit: *Confluence Park (Issaquah):* King County Metro line 271 stops on NW Gilman Boulevard a short distance north of the park.

Walk or run a mostly paved path from one end of massive, glacially scoured Lake Sammamish to the other end—or just sample a small section. A key connector in King County's long-distance trail system, this former rail line runs along the entire eastern shoreline of Lake Sammamish, from Issaquah to Redmond. While houses crowd the shoreline, gaps along the way allow some good lake and Issaquah Alps views—and a couple of parks provide a little natural splendor.

GET MOVING
This former line of the Seattle, Lake Shore, and Eastern Railway had quite a rough start as a trail. King County, intent on converting it to a trail, acquired the corridor in 1998. But some well-heeled adjacent property owners were intent on stopping that from happening. After five years of litigation

battles, the county and trail proponents prevailed. There have been a few more hiccups but now the trail is shaping up quite nicely, with only about 3 miles left to be paved.

While this trail may appeal more to cyclists than to pedestrians, both its southern and northern reaches offer fine walking and running, with access to other trails and parks. The southern and northern reaches also offer breaks from the nearly continuous line of lakeside homes. Below is a general description of the trail from south to north.

From Confluence Park, walk north along Rainier Boulevard N. for 0.2 mile to NW Gilman Boulevard. At a crosswalk just to the west, carefully cross this busy arterial and pick up the start of the trail. The trail parallels 4th Avenue NW, ducks under I-90, and comes to the paved Issaquah-Preston Trail, which parallels I-90. It then reaches the Pickering Trail (see Trail 29). Next, it crosses the North Fork Issaquah Creek and ducks under SE 62nd Street before paralleling E. Lake Sammamish Parkway SE. At 0.8 mile, it crosses busy NW Sammamish Road—then skirts office complexes before entering Lake Sammamish State Park. The trail, now lined with trees and fencing, traverses a scenic, bird-rich wetland before crossing the state park road for the boat launch at 1.8 miles.

The trail then crosses several quiet roads (both private and public) and travels a few local access points. Houses line the way, but some gaps allow for views of the large lake (but no lake access—stay on the trail). The trail eventually pulls away from the parkway, making for more peaceful wandering. At 4.2 miles, it rounds Sulphur Springs Point (the springs are long gone). It then once again parallels the busy parkway, crossing a series of crashing creeks.

At 6.8 miles, the trail passes through the Inglewood section of Sammamish. At 8.7 miles, just north of Weber Point, it travels through the lovely Sammamish Landing Park (parking and restrooms available). While only 8 acres in size, this little park is a highlight along the trail. Take a break at

Trail through Sammamish Landing Park

the park's picnic shelter. Walk its short shoreline trail through mature forest. Dip a toe in sparkling waters at one of the small beaches. And absolutely venture out on one of the two piers to take in one heck of a view. Admire Mount Rainier across the lake, hovering above a gap between Tiger and Squak Mountains. It's breathtaking!

The trail continues north from the park, soon coming to a forested shoreline protected within King County's Marymoor Park. At 10 miles, come to a junction with the Marymoor Connector Trail (see Trail 15). This delightful path traverses Marymoor Park to connect with the Sammamish River Trail (see Trail 2). The East Lake Sammamish Trail continues north, crossing a few roads, skirting businesses, and coming to its northern terminus at NE 70th Street at 10.4 miles.

GO FARTHER

The old rail line continues beyond SR 520 as the Redmond Central Connector Trail (see Trail 15). From its southern terminus, the old rail line continues south beyond Front Street N. as the Rainier Trail. Walk this path through the heart of historic Issaquah, passing interpretive displays, old railroad cars, and historic structures, including one now housing the Issaquah Alps Club. The paved trail runs for 1 mile to 2nd Avenue SE. It then continues as a gravel path, switching back and connecting to the High School Trail leading to Tiger Mountain.

And definitely meander the short but scenic trails within Confluence Park. The bridge spanning Issaquah Creek is an artistic and scenic joy to cross. You'll want to cross it a couple of times.

31 Evans Creek Preserve

DISTANCE:	3.5 miles of trails
ELEVATION GAIN:	Up to 475 feet
HIGH POINT:	500 feet
DIFFICULTY:	Easy to moderate
FITNESS:	Runners, hikers
FAMILY-FRIENDLY:	Yes, including an ADA-accessible trail
DOG-FRIENDLY:	On leash
AMENITIES:	Restrooms, picnic tables
CONTACT/MAPS:	City of Sammamish Parks and Recreation
GPS:	N 47°38.733', W 122°02.455'

GETTING THERE

Driving: From Bellevue, follow I-405 north for 1 mile. Then take the exit for State Route 520 east and drive for 5.9 miles. Take the exit for SR 202 (Redmond Way) and head east (right). Continue for 3.7 miles and turn right onto 224th Avenue NE. Come to the trailhead on your right in 0.1 mile.

Transit: King County Metro line 269 accesses Sahalee Way NE Trailhead.

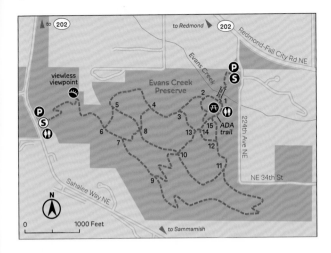

Located within the Evans Creek Valley east of Redmond, this 179-acre preserve was once farm land like much of the valley. City officials recognized this old farm's rich wildlife habitat and its passive recreational values and moved forward to protect it. Take a hike here and be surprised by the preserve's wildness—and catch a glimpse of what much of the Eastside looked like before Microsoft was founded in 1975.

GET MOVING

Unlike many of the other new parks that were recently established in these parts, Evans Creek emphasizes the word "preserve." You won't find many amenities here, or ballparks. No mountain bikes to dodge either—they're prohibited here. What you will find (thanks to the Washington Trails Association) is a well-built network of trails, with signpost maps at each junction. You'll also find meadows, mature forest, lush ravines, and tumbling creeks—all providing exceptional habitat. Deer are common residents, and black bears are occasionally seen here.

Author and son admiring a sloping Western red cedar

From the parking area, a wide trail (formerly a farm road) suitable for wheelchairs and jogging strollers descends about 50 feet to a bridge across Evans Creek. It then emerges at junction number 1 at the edge of a meadow. There are fifteen signed junctions in the preserve—all displaying a map—making orientation easy. The ADA trail makes a small loop along the edge of the meadow, passing a few picnic tables along the way.

Three trails branch off the meadow loop, heading for the woodlands. Weave through groves of big firs and cotton-woods. Another set of trails departs from the woodlands trails—the hillside trails. These trails traverse steep slopes and cross ravine-cradling creeks on sturdy bridges. These hillside trails, with their lush and luxuriant surrounding vegetation, will have you thinking you're somewhere in the Cascades. And you can also get a good little 400-foot climb in by following the trail west from junction number 6 to the trailhead off of Sahalee Way NE. This trailhead is a quieter alternative start for exploring the preserve, but remember you'll have to return and end your hike with a big climb.

Hiking just on the meadow loop is about 0.6 mile. Add a loop with some of the forest trails, and you are looking at 2 miles. Throw the hillside trails in there, and you're over 3 miles. Hike or run all the connector trails as well (which involves some backtracking), and you can easily get a 5-mile workout. The trail map shows some viewpoints, but don't get too excited; they're a mixed bag. The one on the way to the upper trailhead is a real mystery since the view is of thick forest. Despite the occasional oddity, the preserve is quite attractive.

32 Soaring Eagle Regional Park

DISTANCE:	More than 12 miles of trails
ELEVATION GAIN:	Up to 325 feet
HIGH POINT:	550 feet
DIFFICULTY:	Easy to moderate
FITNESS:	Runners, walkers, hikers, cyclists
FAMILY-FRIENDLY:	Yes, but note trails open to mountain bikes and horses
DOG-FRIENDLY:	On leash
AMENITIES:	Restrooms, benches
CONTACT/MAPS:	King County Parks
GPS:	N 47°36.722', W 121°59.464'

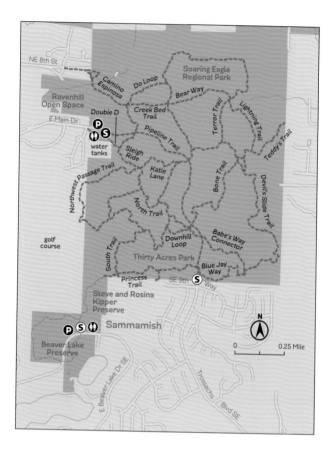

GETTING THERE

Driving: From Bellevue, follow I-405 north for 1 mile. Then take the exit for State Route 520 east and drive for 5.9 miles. Take the exit for SR 202 (Redmond Way) and head east (right). After 5.2 miles, turn right onto 224th Avenue NE. Then drive 2.3 miles and turn left (at the traffic circle) onto E. Main Drive. Continue east 1.1 miles to the park and the trailhead.

Situated on the Sammamish Plateau between a growing city and a tranquil valley, King County's Soaring Eagle Regional Park protects prime woodlands and wetlands. It also provides hikers, runners, and walkers with 12 miles of interconnected, well-built, and well-signed trails. Much of the terrain is pretty gentle, but there are a few dips and rolls along the way. It's a fun place to run and a great place for an easy after-work hike.

GET MOVING

Soaring Eagle Regional Park is a local favorite for trail runners. It's also a favorite place for mountain bikers. While nearby Duthie Hill is the go-to place for serious mountain bikers, Soaring Eagle offers gentler terrain—making it a good spot for beginning, younger, and more sedate bikers. There are plenty of flowy trails, but no terrifying vertical. Much of the park is gently sloping, interspersed with flat spots and small depressions. It's a lot of fun to run, and this park hosts several organized running events each year.

Soaring Eagle was once a Department of Natural Resources tract and as such was logged over the years. The forest is now almost entirely deciduous and feels like it should be in southern New England. Hike, run, or walk here when the trees are bare of their canopy, and it'll feel quite open. In 1993, King County acquired this 600-plus-acre tract for $8 million. Area residents welcomed the new park, but there were some differences over having some of this large, forested tract developed for sports fields. Most of those pressures have thankfully subsided. Soaring Eagle borders two other protected areas, creating an undeveloped swath of more than 800 acres in one of the fastest-growing communities in Washington.

The Pipeline Trail takes off from the parking lot and pretty much bisects the park. Following a waterline, this wide and easy-to-walk (and jogging stroller–friendly) trail drops about 100 feet over its course of 1.2 miles to an alternative trailhead (no facilities) on Trossachs Boulevard SE. From this park "life-line," you can create a lot of loops and routes, as it connects many of the park's trails. The junctions are numbered and well signed.

While much of the Soaring Eagle's terrain is pretty uniform, there is some variation along the park's periphery. The Camino Espinosa (Thorny Path) includes a decent little descent to a large, grassy wetland. Like Teddy's Trail (which also includes a good descent), Camino Espinosa leaves the park for private land. The North Trail and Northwest Passage Trail circle around a large wetland and pass through an attractive cedar grove. The Devil's Slide Trail has little eleva-tion gain and crosses over a small creek. A hike or run along

Well-built trail through wetland

the periphery of the park utilizing many of these trails will yield you 5.5 miles. Not a bad little workout.

GO FARTHER

At junction number 20 in the southwest corner of the park, follow a trail southwest for 0.3 mile through the Steve and Rosina Kipper Preserve to the Beaver Lake Preserve (see Trail 33) for even more trails.

33 Beaver Lake and Hazel Wolf Wetlands Preserves

DISTANCE:	More than 3 miles of trails
ELEVATION GAIN:	Up to 75 feet
HIGH POINT:	475 feet
DIFFICULTY:	Easy
FITNESS:	Walkers, hikers
FAMILY-FRIENDLY:	Yes, some trails stroller- and wheelchair-friendly
DOG-FRIENDLY:	On leash, but prohibited on Ann's Trail
AMENITIES:	Restrooms, benches, interpretive signs, picnic tables
CONTACT/MAPS:	City of Sammamish Parks and Recreation
GPS:	N 47°35.833', W 121°59.486'

GETTING THERE

Driving: From Bellevue, follow I-405 south to I-90 and then head east, taking exit 17. Turn left and drive north on Front Street N., which becomes E. Lake Sammamish Parkway, for 0.4 mile. Turn right onto SE Issaquah-Fall City Road and continue for 3 miles. Then bear left onto SE Duthie Hill Road and drive 0.3 mile. Next turn left onto SE Issaquah Beaver Lake Road and drive 0.5 mile. Then turn right onto E. Beaver Lake Drive SE and proceed 1.7 miles to Beaver Lake Preserve— find parking and the trailhead on your right.

Beautifully built trails traverse these two abutting preserves protecting wildlife-rich wetlands, forests, and lakeshore. Take your time meandering through these placid natural areas, stopping at observation decks along the way. Look for a myriad of birdlife, amphibians, and mammals. And yes, beavers too—their presence is quite pronounced at a large dam.

GET MOVING

Not to be confused with Beaver Lake Park on the west end of the lake, the Beaver Lake Preserve is far more sedate and natural. The former was once a resort and camp—now it's a

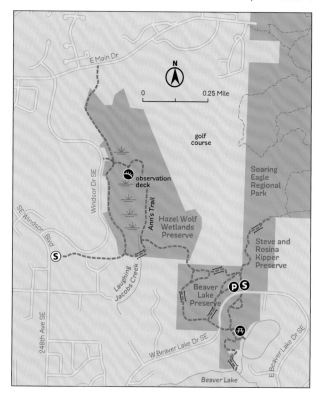

developed and popular park. The latter is a nature preserve with pocket wetlands, stately groves of cedar, and undeveloped shoreline on Beaver Lake. The trail system here is top-notch—built with help from the Washington Trails Association. The trails are wide and smooth and can accommodate jogging strollers and wheelchairs, allowing for this natural area to be enjoyed by outdoor enthusiasts of all ages and abilities. There are a lot of sturdy boardwalks too across this often-saturated landscape—ensuring dry feet.

From the parking lot, you have the choice of making a long loop, several shorter loops, or loops with side trails, short and long. The longest loop is about 1.2 miles, and it involves crossing the road twice. On the south side of the road, you'll come to a picnic area and have a choice of a couple of side trails that lead to shoreline on Beaver Lake. There are interpretive panels throughout the 76-acre preserve, and all the junctions are numbered and marked.

To reach the Hazel Wolf Wetlands, follow a trail off the main loop in the northwest corner of the park. The trail traverses a beautiful grove of mature cedars and enters the 116-acre Hazel Wolf Wetlands Preserve. A passionate activist, environmentalist, and birder, Hazel Wolf was ninety-six years old when this property was preserved by a consortium of public and private interests forged by the Cascade Land Conservancy (now known as Forterra). The preserve was named in her honor on her one hundredth birthday. The preserve is owned and managed by Forterra, one of the largest conservation and land stewardship organizations in the state. Forterra has protected more than 250,000 acres of wildlands, farmlands, and timberlands from development.

You'll soon notice that the trail is now a little rougher than the manicured paths in the Beaver Lake Preserve. At 0.3 mile, you'll come to a junction with Ann's Trail. Dogs are prohibited (so is running) on this trail—so if you have your four-legged hiker with you, you'll need to head back to Beaver Lake. You

Connector trail between Beaver Lake Preserve and Hazel Wolf Wetlands

can go left or right, as Ann's Trail connects with the preserve's main trail to form a 0.7-mile loop around the wetland pool.

The way to the right leads along the eastern shore of the large wetland. It heads out on a boardwalk before arriving at a platform observation deck. There's a good view of Tiger Mountain across the water. Wildlife viewing is excellent too. The trail then comes to a junction with the main trail (dogs allowed on leash). If you follow it right, it eventually crosses part of a golf course and terminates at E. Main Drive in about 0.4 mile.

To complete a loop, head left, traveling through forest wedged between houses and the wetlands' western shore. You'll come to a junction where the main trail leads right 0.3 mile to a neighborhood trailhead (with a small parking area) on SE Windsor Boulevard where it becomes 248th Avenue SE.

You want to go left, back on Ann's Trail. You'll soon come to a large bridged crossing of Laughing Jacobs Creek. Here a large beaver dam is visible to the left and a smaller one can be seen to the right. Just beyond the bridge is the junction with the trail leading back to Beaver Lake.

GO FARTHER
From the Beaver Lake Preserve, you can follow a 0.3-mile trail northeast through the 17-acre Steve and Rosina Kipper Preserve to the 600-plus-acre Soaring Eagle Regional Park (see Trail 32), where 12 more miles of trails await you. All these adjoining parks and preserves create an 800-plus-acre greenbelt.

34 Grand Ridge Park

DISTANCE:	More than 12 miles of trails
ELEVATION GAIN:	Up to 2000 feet
HIGH POINT:	1180 feet
DIFFICULTY:	Moderate
FITNESS:	Hikers, runners, cyclists
FAMILY-FRIENDLY:	Yes, but be aware of heavy mountain-bike use
DOG-FRIENDLY:	On leash
AMENITIES:	Restrooms
CONTACT/MAPS:	King County Parks
GPS:	N 47°34.326', W 121°59.360'

GETTING THERE
Driving: *North Trailhead:* From Bellevue, follow I-405 south to I-90 and then head east, taking exit 17. Turn left and drive north on Front Street N., which becomes E. Lake Sammamish Parkway, for 0.4 mile. Then turn right onto SE Issaquah-Fall City Road and continue for 3 miles. Then bear right, staying on SE Issaquah-Fall City Road, and reach Duthie Hill Trailhead parking on your left in 0.1 mile. *South Trailhead:* From

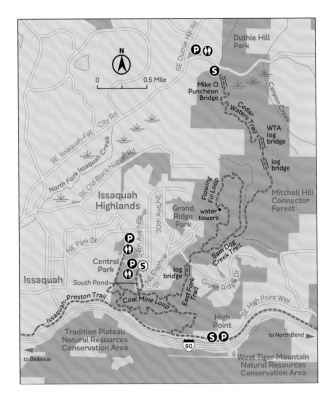

Bellevue, follow I-405 south to I-5 and then head east, taking exit 20 (High Point). Turn left and then immediately after the interchange turn left again into parking area and trailhead.

Transit: *South Trailhead:* King County Metro line 208

Located just north of Tiger Mountain, Grand Ridge acts as a great green wall along the suburban fringe of the Issaquah Highlands. This grand, 1300-acre park along an 1100-foot rolling ridge is a remarkably wild place, rife with wildlife. Grand are its mature cedars and firs, its 12-mile trail system, and

its 600-foot-long boardwalk spanning the wetlands that sur-
round salmon-bearing Canyon Creek.

GET MOVING

While nearby Duthie Hill Park is Grand Central Station for
mountain biking, Grand Ridge sees a fair amount of biker
traffic as well. But this park is also used by horseback riders,
hikers, and trail runners. Grand Ridge's varied terrain is
appealing to hikers and runners, and there are fewer of them
here than on nearby Tiger and Cougar Mountains, making
this park a quieter alternative.

You can get a serious workout if you hike or run an
out-and-back on the East Fork, Sam Dog Creek, and Cedar
Waters Trails (formerly known collectively as the Grand Ridge
Trail), which traverse the ridge north to south for 5.5 miles and
include about 2000 feet of elevation change. A couple of side
trails allow for long loop options both at the north and south
ends of the park. There are a couple of other trailheads in the
park, allowing for various options without having to hike or run
all the trails at once (unless that's your intention).

To do the northern loop, walk a short distance along SE
Issaquah-Fall City Road to the northern terminus of the
Cedar Waters Trail. Then begin descending, coming to the
Mike O Puncheon Bridge. Built by volunteers from the Washington Trails Association (WTA), this sturdy, 600-foot-long
boardwalk bridge is a Grand Ridge highlight. It crosses the
saturated saddle dividing the Issaquah Creek and Canyon
Creek watersheds. The trail then climbs out of the lush
wetland, weaving through groves of big trees and showy
boughs of ferns. It begins a long and well-graded climb and
makes several bridged creek crossings. The trail briefly darts
into the Mitchell Hill Connector Forest, one of several adjacent parks, preserves, and conservation easements making
this greenbelt even grander.

Bridge along the Cedar Waters Trail

The way then slightly descends, reaching a junction with the Flowing Fir Loop (formerly known as the Water Tower Loop Trail) at 3.1 miles. Here you can go left on the Sam Dog Creek Trail or right on the loop for a long and flowy but gentle climb up and over the ridge's highest points, passing a pair of water towers. The trail then returns to the Sam Dog Creek Trail after 2.4 miles, from where it is 0.5 mile east (left) back to the previous junction. Return to your start for a 9.1-mile lollipop loop adventure.

To do the southern loop, begin from the High Point Trailhead. Walk west on the Issaquah-Preston Trail (an old railroad line) for 0.6 mile, coming to the southern terminus of the East Fork Trail. Then begin climbing away from the freeway. Winter wren song soon replaces the buzz of automobiles. At 1.3 miles (after 300 feet of climbing), reach a junction with the Coal Mine Loop. This trail winds and drops and climbs again, crossing a couple of creeks to make a 2.1-mile loop. It reaches the East Fork Trail 0.25 mile north of its first junction with it. Return right for a hike just shy of 5 miles.

The Coal Mine Loop offers other variations too. After 0.7 mile from the first junction, a small spur connects with the Issaquah-Preston Trail—from here it is about 1 mile west back to the trailhead. At 1.3 miles and 1.7 miles, a trail departs north to Issaquah's Central Park (alternative trailhead, restrooms), where you can hike a small loop around South Pond. And if you're looking for more mileage and variations, you can continue north on East Fork Trail from the Coal Mine Loop's second junction with it for 0.8 mile to the Flowing Fir Loop and add that trail to your lineup.

Next page: *Mossy bridge crossing in the Many Creeks Valley (Trail 47)*

ISSAQUAH ALPS

Coined by legendary guidebook author and conservationist Harvey Manning (see sidebar "Cougar Mountain's Curmudgeonly Conservationist"), the Issaquah Alps were once the domain of loggers and miners. But due in no small measure to Manning's dogged advocacy, today these Cascade foothills comprise one of the largest urban wildlands in America. The Issaquah Alps consist primarily of Cougar Mountain, Squak Mountain, Tiger Mountain, Rattlesnake Mountain, and to a lesser degree, Taylor Mountain. Laced with one of the largest and best-maintained trail systems in the country, they sit within an hour's drive (when traffic is moving) of more than four million people. Not surprisingly, some of these trails are among the most used in the state. But crowding tends to occur on just a handful of them, leaving many other trails quiet—and it's not uncommon to find even some solitude among these peaks.

The lowest of the Issaquah Alps, Cougar Mountain is also the closest to Seattle and the most interesting when it comes to human history. Long home to Native peoples, early Euro Americans settled here to establish flourishing coal and logging industries. In the 1950s and early '60s, the US military ran an antiaircraft center on the mountain, complete with missile silos. In 1985, King County established the Cougar Mountain Regional Wildland Park—and it has grown to more than 3100 acres, including more than 40 miles of interconnected trails. Some are shared with horses, but none are open to bikes, making this a place where foot traffic rules.

Situated between the very popular Tiger and Cougar Mountains, 2024-foot Squak Mountain is often overlooked by area hikers. This makes Squak an excellent choice for avoiding crowds, and there are about 20 miles of trails here to get away from it all. Washington State Parks manages nearly 1600 acres on the mountain while King County Parks owns more than 700 acres. And as far as Squak's unique name, the late great trail advocate Ruth Ittner once told me, "If you were stuck between a tiger and cougar, you'd squawk too!" Actually, the name means "snake" (which also makes many a hiker squawk) in a local Native dialect and was the original name of the city of Issaquah.

Undoubtedly the king of the Issaquah Alps, Tiger Mountain actually consists of several peaks, with the tallest, East Tiger Mountain, exceeding 3000 feet. The brunt of it lies within the Washington Department of Natural Resources's (DNR) 13,745-acre Tiger Mountain State Forest. And while a good portion of Tiger Mountain is a working forest open to logging, more than 4,400 acres of the forest is set aside as a Natural Resources Conservation Area (NRCA).

There are more than 60 miles of trails on Tiger Mountain. Nearly all of the trails within East Tiger Mountain are managed primarily for mountain biking. While they are also open to hiking, I have left them out of this book as they are too biker busy to enjoy by foot. As far as tigers on Tiger Mountain? The name could be a reference to cougars. The mountain was once known as Issaquah Mountain, and there has been some interest as of late to bestow the mountain with its original name.

The least known of the Issaquah Alps, Taylor Mountain lies between Tiger Mountain and the closed-to-the-public City of Seattle Cedar River Municipal Watershed Ecological Reserve. King County's Taylor Mountain Forest protects nearly 2000 acres on the mountain's southwest slopes. Its more than 20 miles of trails are favored by area equestrians but also offer uncrowded hiking and trail running experiences.

Rattlesnake Mountain tops in at over 3500 feet, making it the highest of the Issaquah Alps. Most hikers know this broad, long mountain primarily for its highly scenic ledges. Those ledges are popular and can get downright crowded—but Rattlesnake contains more than 10 miles of other trails that are often quiet. A consortium of government agencies manage nearly 1800 acres on the mountain as a scenic area. Rattlesnake also borders Raging River State Forest, which has become a premier location for mountain biking since the new trail system opened in 2018.

These five mountains and their satellite ridges, knolls, hillocks, and valleys form more than 25,000 acres of publicly protected lands—and growing. State, county, and municipal governments, as well as an array of conservation groups—including the Issaquah Alps Trails Club, Mountains to Sound Greenway (see sidebar "Preserving a Landscape from Mountains to Sound"), and Forterra (formerly known as the Cascade Land Conservancy)—have been instrumental in protecting these peaks.

ISSAQUAH ALPS: COUGAR MOUNTAIN

35 De Leo Wall

DISTANCE:	4.8 miles roundtrip
ELEVATION GAIN:	475 feet
HIGH POINT:	1119 feet
DIFFICULTY:	Moderate
FITNESS:	Hikers, runners
FAMILY-FRIENDLY:	Yes
DOG-FRIENDLY:	On leash
AMENITIES:	Privies, picnic tables, interpretive signs
CONTACT/MAPS:	King County Parks; Green Trails Cougar Mountain/ Squak Mountain No. 203S
BEFORE YOU GO:	Parking lot is open 8:00 AM to dusk
GPS:	N 47°32.120', W 122°07.711'

GETTING THERE

Driving: From Bellevue, follow I-405 south and take exit 10. Turn left onto Coal Creek Parkway SE and continue south for 1.4 miles. Turn left on Forest Drive SE and continue for 2.1 miles. Next, turn right onto Lakemont Boulevard SE and drive 0.5 mile to the trailhead and parking on your left. The trailhead can also be accessed from exit 13 on I-90 by driving 3.2 miles south on Lakemont Boulevard SE.

Explore the remains of an old mining town, an old mine shaft, and a recovering meadow before setting out on a loop up and over a prominent peak in the Newcastle Hills. Marvel at large, stately trees and stand upon a point granting views out to Mount Rainier and Lake Washington. And if this route isn't enough, there are so many add-on choices at your command—a small waterfall, an old dam, a historic military road, and more.

GET MOVING

This is the busiest corner of the sprawling Cougar Mountain Regional Wildland Park, but crowds thin out considerably once you're beyond the park's old town sites and Coal Creek Falls (see Trail 36). Start by walking on a former road—the Red Town Trail (W2). All trail numbers at Cougar Mountain are preceded with either a C, E, N, S, or W, corresponding to their general location within the sprawling park: central, east, north, south, or west. This helps when you are out on a long hike or run. But be sure to always have a map along with you, lest you end up in an end of the park you weren't planning on visiting at the moment.

The Red Town Trail travels through the site of a long-gone coal-mining company town. All the homes here were painted red. Contrast that with nearby Rainbow Town, another defunct company town whose homes were painted in a wide array of colors. You can learn about these settlements and the industry that gave them birth by taking side trips on the short Bagley Seam Trail (W10), Rainbow Town Trail (W3), and Steam Hoist Trail (W4), which all branch from this loop. The Rainbow Town Trail includes the Ford Slope coal-mining exhibit, where you can view a mine entrance (the largest producer of the Newcastle mines) and a coal cart.

Red Town Trail continues south on a near-level course, crossing Coal Creek and coming to a short loop trail skirting a meadow that was once used as a ballfield for company baseball games. It's now restored, with native vegetation. Check it out, then come to a junction at 0.8 mile. Continue left on the Indian Trail (W7)—or go straight on Marshall's Hill Trail (W6) if you want just a short loop around Red Town.

Now follow another old road-turned-trail on a near-level course along Long Marsh, coming to a junction at 1.4 miles. You'll be heading west here on the De Leo Wall Trail (W9), but feel free to head left for a short side diversion (0.25 mile roundtrip) to nearby Far Country Falls if you'd like. The De Leo Wall Trail traverses a hillside and then begins to climb, reaching a junction at 1.8 miles. Here the official trail heads right—but you may want to head left first, following a path 0.2 mile to the De Leo Wall viewpoint, just outside of the park. Here find a small ledge (keep dogs and children nearby) with a good view out to Mount Rainier and Lake Washington.

Coal cart at the Red Town site

There are also two other trails here—one leading steeply north back to the main loop, the other leading west and connecting with the East Cross Town Trail (see Trail 24). This trail has some good viewpoints but can be treacherous with its steep ledges. This area was recently threatened with clear-cut logging—not a wise choice for a steep, unstable hillside. In 2019 concerned citizens and conservationists were able to protect this property and add it to the park (where it belongs).

After soaking up the view, retrace your steps back to the main route and then turn left, steeply climbing up to the 1119-foot summit of Marshall's Hill. The trees here are old and

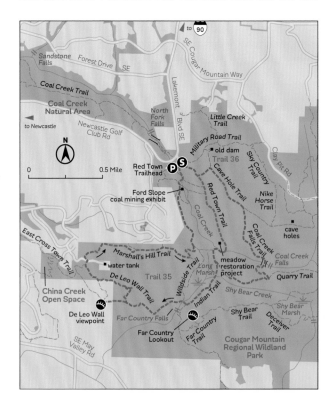

tall. Now pass a path coming up from De Leo Wall and then start descending, coming to a junction at 2.9 miles. Here the East Cross Town Trail heads west to Newcastle. You want to continue right, now on the Marshall's Hill Trail (W6).

Cross an access road for a water tower and skirt a neighborhood as you continue to descend through attractive forest. At 4.1 miles, come to a junction with the Wildside Trail (W1). Take this old road-turned-trail left, passing through Red Town and side trails before crossing over Coal Creek and returning to your start at 4.8 miles.

GO FARTHER

In addition to exploring all the short trails around Red Town, consider a hike up the Military Road Trail (N2) to the Red Town Creek Trail and an old dam site, or the new Sky Country Trail, leading to a trailhead of the same name. You can then return to Red Town via the Cave Hole Trail for a loop of about 2.5 miles.

36 Coal Creek Falls

DISTANCE:	2.5 miles roundtrip
ELEVATION GAIN:	600 feet
HIGH POINT:	1100 feet
DIFFICULTY:	Easy
FITNESS:	Hikers, runners
FAMILY-FRIENDLY:	Yes
DOG-FRIENDLY:	On leash
AMENITIES:	Privies, picnic tables, benches, interpretive signs
CONTACT/MAPS:	King County Parks; Green Trails Cougar Mountain/ Squak Mountain No. 203S
BEFORE YOU GO:	Parking lot is open 8:00 AM to dusk and fills up fast on sunny weekends
GPS:	N 47°32.120', W 122°07.711'

Coal Creek Falls in a mossy ravine

GETTING THERE

Driving: From Bellevue, follow I-405 south and take exit 10. Then turn left onto Coal Creek Parkway SE and continue south for 1.4 miles. Turn left on Forest Drive SE and continue for 2.1 miles. Next, turn right onto Lakemont Boulevard SE and drive 0.5 mile to the trailhead and parking on your left. The trailhead can also be accessed from exit 13 on I-90 by driving 3.2 miles south on Lakemont Boulevard SE.

One of the crown jewels of sprawling Cougar Mountain Regional Wildland Park, it's not surprising Coal Creek Falls is also one of the park's most popular destinations. Hikers of all ages and abilities can make the trip to the 28-foot cascade tumbling over mossy ledges. A near trickle in late summer, the falls are especially delightful when autumn rains have swelled the creek and golden maple leaves brighten the surrounding emerald gorge.

GET MOVING

Head up the wide, old road now known as Red Town Trail (W2). If you haven't explored what remains of the old coal-mining settlement of Red Town, plan on doing so after you visit the falls. After 0.2 mile come to a junction. Here another old road-turned-trail, the Cave Hole Trail (C3), takes off left. Take it—you'll be returning on the trail to the right.

Cave Hole Trail steadily climbs. It was named for sinkholes in the ground surface caused by years of underground coal mining—there are quite a few of them farther up the trail and throughout the park. Some have been filled in, others have collected water, and others remain large depressions. They are all potentially dangerous and should never be entered.

At 0.6 mile come to a junction (elev. 1050 feet) with the Coal Creek Falls Trail (C4). You guessed it—follow it right. This well-trodden trail traverses a hillside before descending

COUGAR MOUNTAIN'S CURMUDGEONLY CONSERVATIONIST

Harvey Manning and Ira Spring were two of the greatest advocates and stewards for Washington's trails and wild places. Through their words and photography in a myriad of groundbreaking books, they introduced thousands to hiking. More importantly, they educated and alerted the public—and rallied them to protect so many of those wild places that were threatened with logging, mining, development, motorized use, and other incompatible activities.

Manning was born in Seattle in 1925 and spent a good part of his life living on Cougar Mountain. He was an avid hiker, backpacker, and climber and a prolific writer. Mountaineers Books was founded as a division of The Mountaineers in 1953, largely due to Manning. In 1960 they published their first book, the seminal *Mountaineering: The Freedom of the Hills*. It's largely regarded as the bible of hiking, with more than 750,000 copies sold.

Manning was also an ardent conservationist, leaving quite a green legacy behind. He was both eloquent and outspoken and was fiercely committed to protecting our wild places. Among Manning's many environmental achievements was his cofounding of the North Cascades Conservation Council (NCCC), which advocated for a North Cascades National Park (finally coming to fruition in 1968). He was also founder of the Issaquah Alps Trails Club, which promotes sound recreation and conservation on the largest tracts of state and county lands just to the east of Seattle. He worked hard to make these places friendly and accessible to hikers (he was no fan of mountain bikes and motorcycles).

Manning passed away in 2006 at eighty-one, three years after Spring passed away at the age of eighty-four. Though curmudgeonly and polarizing at times, he had a huge impact on me as a writer and a conservationist. King County Parks honored Manning by renaming a major trailhead and popular trail on Cougar Mountain after him. The City of Issaquah named a new park and erected a statue in his honor in front of the Issaquah Trails Center (headquarters of the Issaquah Alps Club). No doubt Manning would have hated the statue and not wanted any part of it.

150 feet into a mossy, ferny ravine. Your ears will let you know you are getting close to the falls. At 1 mile reach a bridge (elev. 900 feet) spanning Coal Creek just below the showy falls. Stay for a while and try to capture the cascade on pixels.

Once content, continue across the bridge and climb out of the ravine, reaching a junction (elev. 1100 feet) at 1.2 miles with the Quarry Trail (C6). Now hike this road-turned-trail right, descending alongside Shy Bear Creek and reaching the Indian Trail (W7) at 1.6 miles. Turn right here on yet another road-turned-trail and enjoy a relaxing near-level return to your start. Pass the Long Marsh to your left and come to a junction with the Marshall's Hill Trail (see Trail 35) at 1.7 miles. Go right. The Indian Trail bends left, crosses Coal Creek, and becomes the Red Town Trail (W2). Here too is a short loop leading left to a restored meadow once used as a ballfield for the former mining communities located just up the road-trail.

Continue on the Red Town Trail, returning to your start at 2.5 miles. En route you'll pass the Rainbow Town Trail (W3) and Bagley Seam Trail (W10) leading left. These two short trails are full of history and artifacts from Cougar's coal-mining days and should not be missed if you have never hiked them before. From either one you can make a loop, returning to the trailhead via either the China Creek Trail (W5) or Wildside Trail (W1).

GO FARTHER

Expand your loop by a mile to include the Far Country Falls. Follow the Indian Trail left to the falls, and then return the same way (or via the Wildside Trail). The falls are pretty—but if you visit during the drier months, you won't be wowing.

37 Anti-Aircraft Peak Loop

DISTANCE:	4.4 miles roundtrip
ELEVATION GAIN:	500 feet
HIGH POINT:	1483 feet
DIFFICULTY:	Moderate
FITNESS:	Hikers, runners
FAMILY-FRIENDLY:	Yes
DOG-FRIENDLY:	On leash
AMENITIES:	Privies, picnic tables, interpretive signs
CONTACT/MAPS:	King County Parks; Green Trails Cougar Mountain/ Squak Mountain No. 203S
BEFORE YOU GO:	Parking lot is open 8:00 AM to dusk
GPS:	N 47°31.983', W 122°06.820'

GETTING THERE

Driving: From Bellevue, follow I-405 south and take exit 10. Then turn left onto Coal Creek Parkway SE and continue south for 1.4 miles. Turn left on Forest Drive SE and continue for 2.1 miles. Next, turn left onto Lakemont Boulevard SE and drive 0.2 mile. Then turn right onto SE Cougar Mountain Way and drive 0.6 mile. Turn right onto 166th Way SE (which becomes Clay Pit Road) and proceed 0.7 mile to the Sky Country Trailhead. The trailhead can also be accessed from exit 13 on I-90 by driving 2.3 miles south on Lakemont Boulevard SE, turning left on SE Cougar Mountain Way, and then following the directions above.

Explore the heart of sprawling Cougar Mountain Regional Wildland Park on this loop (see Trial 38 for map), which includes fascinating history; a large, unintentional marsh; and a million-dollar view. Walk into the past to when this area was influenced by coal mining and the Cold War. Wander through

Big trees near the Klondike Marsh

the remnants of a long-gone military installation that housed Nike missiles and walk part of a red-brick road.

GET MOVING

Several trails branch from the large Sky Country Trailhead parking lot. You can assemble quite a few loops here—short and long. Feel free to abbreviate or lengthen this suggested one. Locate the Old Man's Trail (C11) heading east and immediately come to a structure that looks like an old bus stop shelter near large, concrete circles in a field. Welcome to the remains of a Nike missile launch site that occupied this spot from 1957 to 1964. Built to stop an enemy aircraft attack, this launch site was one of several located around the Seattle area during the Cold War. The radar installation which controlled this silo was atop Anti-Aircraft Peak—coming up on your loop.

Continue on Old Man's Trail and pass a fenced-in cave hole. There are scores of these around this area of Cougar Mountain. Remnants of the coal-mining era, these were formed where the ground surface collapsed due to underground mining. Many have been filled. Some now house wetlands. All are dangerous and should not be entered. Come to the Cave Hole Trail (C3) at 0.2 mile. Turn left and at 0.3 mile come to the Clay Pit Road (C1) and Coyote Creek Trail. You'll be returning on that trail, so head right on the now-closed-to-traffic Clay Pit Road, soon crossing North Fork Coal Creek below a beaver dam at the head of massive Klondike Marsh. This wildlife-rich marsh was once a mill pond for coal operations downstream in Newcastle. Logging on surrounding hills in the early twentieth century lead to the pond filling with silt, transforming it into a marsh.

At 0.5 mile come to a junction where the 0.8-mile Klondike Swamp Trail (N5) heads left and can be followed to shorten this loop. Alternatively, Fred's Railroad Trail (C7) leads right and can be followed 0.3 mile to the 0.7-mile East Fork Trail (C8) to the 0.3-mile Mine Shaft Trail (C10) for a longer loop. Continue east on the road, climbing on a near-straight course. At 0.8 mile come to a junction with the Mine Shaft Trail. Walk down it for 0.1 mile to a huge, covered mine air shaft, and read about the shaft at the adjacent kiosk. Then return to the road and continue right 0.1 mile to a junction with the Protector Trail (N9) near the road's end (elev. 1375 feet) at an old clay pit (quarry).

Did you notice all the bricks embedded in the road? This defunct clay pit was used by the Mutual Materials Company for more than fifty years. The clay here was fired into bricks at their Newcastle factory; these bricks were used all over the Northwest, including the University of Washington's Red Square. The clay pit closed in 2015 and remains closed to the public as King County Parks works on restoring it to a natural state.

Now turn left on the Protector Trail and wind down to a junction. Here at 1.3 miles the Protector Trail continues right to Tibbetts Marsh (see Trail 38). You want to go left on the Cougar Pass Trail (N8) for 0.2 mile and then turn right

onto the Harvey Manning Trail (N7). Follow this well-trav-
eled trail through mature forest, gently climbing up a ridge
and coming to a junction with the Lost Beagle Trail (N6) at
2.2 miles.

You'll be heading left—but first continue on the Harvey
Manning Trail another 0.1 mile to the Harvey Manning Trailhead (alternative start) and then another 0.1 mile to the
Million Dollar View to enjoy a great view out to Lake Sammamish from this high point. Read all about Manning too (see
sidebar "Cougar Mountain's Curmudgeonly Conservationist"),
who was responsible for this park's creation. Then retrace
your steps and continue hiking east on the Lost Beagle Trail,
climbing to the top of 1483-foot Anti-Aircraft Peak.

Locate a gap in the old fence allowing access to the
towered summit; it's surrounded by sidewalks, steps, and
roads but no structures from the former radar command
center for the missile silos you passed earlier. This site once
housed antiaircraft guns too, before the missile silos were
built. If you want to roam around the grassy grounds to the
west, feel free—and stop at the historic displays scattered
about. Otherwise keep hiking, descending to a junction with
the Klondike Swamp Trail at 3.3 miles.

Head right and in 0.1 mile come to the Coyote Creek
Trail. Then turn left, skirting the massive Klondike Marsh and
coming to Clay Pit Road at a familiar junction at 4.2 miles.
Turn right, returning to your start in 0.2 mile.

GO FARTHER

Circle around Anti-Aircraft Peak on the Shangri La Trail to
Coyote Creek Trail. Take the new Sky Country Trail east from
the parking lot to the Military Road Trail—then follow that trail
left to the Red Town Creek Trail, passing the old Red Town
Dam Site. Return to your start by following the Cave Hole
Trail to Clay Pit Road, passing many cave holes along the
way. This loop is about 2.2 miles.

38 Big Tree Ridge

DISTANCE:	4.4 miles roundtrip
ELEVATION GAIN:	1350 feet
HIGH POINT:	1430 feet
DIFFICULTY:	Difficult
FITNESS:	Hikers, runners
FAMILY-FRIENDLY:	Yes
DOG-FRIENDLY:	On leash
AMENITIES:	None
CONTACT/MAPS:	King County Parks; Green Trails Cougar Mountain/ Squak Mountain No. 203S
BEFORE YOU GO:	Parking lot is open 8:00 AM to dusk
GPS:	N 47°32.804', W 122°04.214'

GETTING THERE

Driving: From Bellevue, follow I-405 south and take exit 15. Then turn right onto 17th Avenue NW and drive 0.4 mile. Turn right and proceed 0.5 mile on Newport Way NW to the trailhead and parking, located on your left.

One of Cougar Mountain's newest trails, Big Tree Ridge is surprisingly also one of its quietest. Follow this well-built trail right from Issaquah up a steep ridge, passing—you guessed it—big trees along the way. Enjoy teaser views of Lake Sammamish and a grand view of the lake and beyond if you push all the way to Anti-Aircraft Peak (see Trail 37). And if you want to wander, there are several excellent loops you can do after the initial climb.

GET MOVING

The Big Tree Ridge Trail (E16) travels up a narrow strip of park land between developments of big homes that continue to inch up higher on the unprotected eastern slopes of Cougar Mountain. Large, undeveloped tracts in this area still exist and would make better park additions than home sites on these steep, unstable slopes. But money talks loudly here, where housing demands are strong and real estate prices are astronomical. Conservationists continue to fight to protect the integrity of this backyard wilderness.

Start in scrappy forest that will someday recover, and cross a small creek. Then begin to climb, steeply switchbacking up a ridge that soon sports big, old, attractive trees: Douglas firs, western hemlocks, western red cedars, and grand firs. The trail works its way up a rib between two ravines cradling cascading creeks. Nearby freeway noise, however, drowns out much of the music streaming below. Pause to take in a couple of good views out over Lake Sammamish.

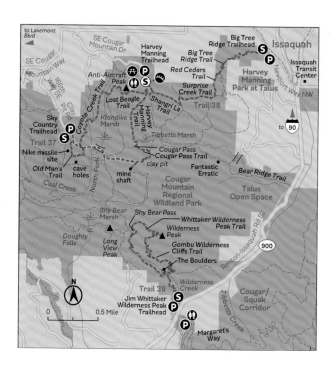

Lake Sammamish from the Million Dollar View

At 0.4 mile come to a junction (elev. 450 feet) with a trail leading 0.5 mile to Harvey Manning Park (not to be confused with the Harvey Manning Trailhead) in the Talus neighborhood. This trail (as well as forest surrounding it) may be severely impacted if a controversial proposed development moves forward.

Keep right and keep climbing, coming to another junction (elev. 725 feet) at 0.9 mile. Here the Military Ridge Trail (E14) takes off left to the Precipice Top Trail (E13). The Military Ridge Trail continues to private property. The Precipice Top Trail, recently rerouted because of a new development, travels 0.3 mile to the Surprise Creek Trail (E2) and makes for a nice alternative return route. The Big Tree Ridge Trail bends right and becomes the Red Cedars Trail (E12). Continue on it, coming to a junction (elev. 900 feet) with the Surprise Creek Trail at 1.2 miles.

Then head right on the Surprise Creek Trail, which is actually an old road and easy to walk. Stay right at the No Name Trail (E8) junction and left at the Goode's Corner Trail (E7)—the former offering an alternative return and the latter leading out of the park. At 1.7 miles, come to a junction (elev. 1230 feet) with the Shangri La Trail (E1). You want to take this old, wide road-trail right, steadily climbing and passing the Harvey Manning Trail on your left and reaching the Harvey Manning Trailhead parking area (elev. 1430 feet) at 2.1 miles.

Now definitely walk the short, 0.1-mile path right to the Pergola Viewpoint, also known as the Million Dollar View. Directly below you is Lake Sammamish—and beyond, Mount Baker. Nod a friendly hello to folks casually walking up to the viewpoint after driving to the nearby parking lot. You certainly earned this view, million dollars or not!

GO FARTHER

You have many options to extend your hike or run instead of settling for a straight out-and-back. Combine with the Anti-Aircraft Peak Loop (see Trail 37). Or add on a 2-mile loop around Tibbets Marsh by following the Harvey Manning Trail (N7) to the Cougar Pass Trail (N8) to the Tibbetts Marsh Trail (N9)—or shorten that loop by taking the 0.3-mile Protector Trail (E9) back to the Shangri La Trail instead.

Consider checking out the big, fern-topped Fantastic Erratic, one of the biggest glacial erratics in the Issaquah Alps. To reach it, follow the delightful 0.4-mile West Tibbetts Creek Trail (E10) from the Tibbetts Marsh Trail (N9) to the Bear Ridge Trail (E3). Then hike right on this trail, dropping 200 feet and reaching the big boulder in 0.4 mile. You can return by following the Bear Ridge Trail 0.6 mile to the Shangri La Trail. Head 0.1 mile left and then go right on the No Name Trail 0.2 mile back to the Surprise Creek Trail.

The Fantastic Erratic can also be reached by following the Bear Ridge Trail from a small trailhead on State Route 900 (1.4 miles south of exit 15). This lightly hiked trail traverses the city of Issaquah's Talus Open Space lands, passing the Talus Bridge Trail leading to the Talus development and reaching the erratic in 0.9 mile.

39   Wilderness Peak Loop

DISTANCE:	3.9 miles roundtrip
ELEVATION GAIN:	1200 feet
HIGH POINT:	1598 feet
DIFFICULTY:	Difficult
FITNESS:	Hikers, runners
FAMILY-FRIENDLY:	Yes
DOG-FRIENDLY:	On leash
AMENITIES:	Privy, picnic tables, benches, kiosk, map box
CONTACT/MAPS:	King County Parks; Green Trails Cougar Mountain/ Squak Mountain No. 203S
BEFORE YOU GO:	Parking lot is open 8:00 AM to dusk. Warning: car break-ins frequently occur at this trailhead—do not leave valuables in your vehicle.
GPS:	N 47°30.610', W 122°05.260'

GETTING THERE

Driving: From Bellevue, follow I-405 south to I-90 and then head east, taking exit 15 in Issaquah. Turn right (south) onto State Route 900 (17th Avenue NW) and proceed for 3.2 miles. Then turn right into the Jim Whittaker Wilderness Peak Trailhead and parking. Additional parking is available across the road at the Cougar/Squak Corridor parking lot.

From Renton, follow I-405 north to exit 5. Turn right and drive SR 900 (NE Park Drive, which becomes NE Sunset Boulevard) for 6.2 miles. Then turn right into the wilderness trailhead and parking. Additional parking is available across the road at the Cougar/Squak Corridor parking lot.

Transit: King County Metro Trailhead Direct shuttle (seasonal) at the Cougar/Squak Corridor parking lot across the road.

Hike to Cougar Mountain's highest summit. Just shy of 1600 feet, it's no Everest—but its trails are named in honor of two men who have summited the world's highest peak. And while Wilderness Peak may not exactly be true wilderness, this rugged corner of King County's largest park has the least amount of past human impact. You won't get any views—but you'll hike through old-growth forest and along a cascading creek, and you'll get a good workout.

GET MOVING

One of the tougher trips on Cougar Mountain—surprisingly, this is also one of the more popular ones. You'll encounter trail runners, hikers training for future big ascents, and folks of all abilities and experiences, including ones who had no idea what they were getting themselves into.

It's a lollipop loop starting on the Whittaker Wilderness Peak Trail (E6). The trail and the beautiful bridge spanning tumbling Wilderness Creek is named in honor of Seattle native Jim Whittaker, who in 1963 became the first American to summit Mount Everest.

Steadily climbing through a ferny fairyland, weave your way through mature second-growth trees adorned with clumps of ferns, and scoot around giant fern-topped boulders. The trail works its way up a steep ridge, pulling away from the cascading creek. The soothing water music, however, is oft out-played by the industrial music coming from a nearby quarry.

At 0.5 mile cross the creek on a bridge once more, coming to a junction (elev. 875 feet) at an area called The Boulders for obvious reasons. Now for the loop. I find going counter-clockwise easier, subduing the steepest part first. So head right on the Gombu Wilderness Cliffs Trail (E5)—named in honor of Nawang Gombu, a Sherpa who summited Mount Everest with Whittaker. Gombu's uncle was Tenzing Norgay; in 1953, Norgay and Sir Edmund Hillary became the first two human souls to climb the world's tallest mountain.

Bridge over Wilderness Creek

At 0.6 mile come to another junction. The trail straight ahead is the very lightly hiked Squak Mountain Connector Trail (E11). It travels downhill, mainly on an old road, coming to SR 900 in 0.7 mile. From there it's a short walk on the road left to Squak's West Access Trail. You want to continue left on the Gombu Trail, negotiating a series of steep switchbacks. The way then travels along a series of mossy ledges. Don't believe maps showing a viewpoint—it, like many in the park, has grown in.

A second round of switchbacks soon greets you, taking you through groves of some of the biggest and oldest trees on Cougar Mountain. Pass a small wetland and make one more uphill charge, coming to a junction at 1.8 miles. The spur (E4) right leads 0.1 mile to Wilderness Peak's 1598-foot summit. Take it to say you've done it. No views—just a bench among some big trees. Continue on the main way, moderately losing elevation and coming to Shy Bear (the kind you'd want to meet along the way) Pass (elev. 1375 feet) at 2.4 miles.

The Shy Bear Trail goes right—you want to head left. Then head left again on the Whittaker Trail, where the Long View

Peak Trail leads right. The Whittaker Trail steeply descends through beautiful old-growth, coming to a hanging valley of big, mossy maples, cedars, and boulders. Cross Wilderness Creek on a boardwalk and then hike above it as the creek cuts through a gorge. The trail eventually steeply drops to cross the creek and return to the The Boulders junction at 3.4 miles. Now head right for 0.5 mile on familiar tread, returning to your start.

GO FARTHER

Extend this loop by following the Long View Peak Trail (S4)—where the view is long gone—to the Deceiver Trail (S3) and returning right on the Shy Bear Trail. Highlights include Doughty Falls (showy in winter—not so much in summer) and Shy Bear Marsh (peaceful year round and mosquitoey in the summer). This loop adds 2.2 miles, about 600 feet of elevation, and a good chance for solitude.

ISSAQUAH ALPS: SQUAK MOUNTAIN

40 Bullitt Fireplace

DISTANCE:	3.6 miles roundtrip
ELEVATION GAIN:	1200 feet
HIGH POINT:	1900 feet
DIFFICULTY:	Moderate
FITNESS:	Hikers, runners
FAMILY-FRIENDLY:	Yes
DOG-FRIENDLY:	On leash
AMENITIES:	Picnic table
CONTACT/MAPS:	King County Parks; Green Trails Cougar Mountain/ Squak Mountain No. 203S
GPS:	N 47°31.381', W 122°03.453'

GETTING THERE

Driving: From Bellevue, follow I-405 south to I-90 and then head east, taking exit 15 in Issaquah. Turn right (south) onto State Route 900 (17th Avenue NW) and proceed for 0.3 mile. Then turn left onto NW Maple Street and continue 0.5 mile to where the arterial bends right and becomes Newport Way NW. Stay on Newport Way NW for 1 mile. Then turn right onto Mountain Park Boulevard SW and follow it for 0.9 mile. Bear right onto Mountainside Drive SW and proceed for 0.4 mile to the trailhead, located on your right at a sharp curve. Park on the wide road shoulder.

Follow an old road—now a quiet, forested track—to the remains of a summer cabin high on Squak Mountain. There are no sweeping views, waterfalls, or cathedral forests. Just a peaceful, lightly traveled path through a mountain refuge in a sea of encroaching suburbanization. Priceless. And if 3.6 miles to and from a fireplace in the forest is not enough to soothe your soul and raise your heartbeat—there are miles of side trails to explore.

GET MOVING

The Bullitt Fireplace is one of the more popular destinations on this quiet Issaquah Alp. The tall, impressive stone fireplace is in essence the heart of Squak Mountain and where all of this surrounding protected land originated. In 1952, attorney Stimson Bullitt of Seattle's prominent Bullitt family built a summer cottage on Squak after purchasing nearly 600 acres of land on the mountain. His wife wasn't very fond of it, and the cottage saw little use, eventually succumbing to vandalism. All that remains of the cottage is the fireplace and foundation.

In line with the Bullitt family's strong environmental and philanthropic ethos, Stimson's children donated their entire landholding on the mountain to Washington State Parks in 1972, with the stipulation that it remain undeveloped and wild.

Through subsequent purchases, the state park now totals nearly 1600 acres. Adjacent King County and Issaquah park and conservation lands bring the total protected area on this mountain to more than 3000 acres.

Starting at an elevation of 740 feet, the Bullitt Fireplace Trailhead is Squak's highest trailhead. The trail follows the old road that was used to access the cabin. It traverses a steep hillside through a forest of hemlock, maple, and Douglas fir. Gaps in the forest canopy—particularly in the winter months—provide some limited views north to Lake Sammamish. At 0.5 mile come to a junction. Here the Coal Mine Trail heads right 0.2 mile, passing old mine depressions before reaching the West Access Trail.

Continue left on the Bullitt Fireplace Trail, skirting a housing development before bending south and entering the state park. At 1 mile reach a junction—the West Access Trail leads right; the East Side Trail leads left. You want to continue straight, gaining more elevation. At 1.4 miles, bear left at the

Bullitt Fireplace

junction with the Chybinski Loop Trail. At 1.6 miles, pass the Bullitt Gorge Trail coming up from the right. At 1.8 miles, reach the fireplace (elev. 1900 feet) in a small opening in the forest. A picnic table invites you to take a break. After lounging, return the way you came—or consider the options below for a longer hike.

GO FARTHER

You can continue following the Bullitt Fireplace Trail for 0.3 mile beyond the fireplace. It descends about 100 feet and reaches a junction with the Central Peak Trail. From here it is 0.3 mile right to the 2024-foot towered and viewless Central Peak—or 0.6 mile left back to the Bullitt Fireplace Trail, offering a lollipop loop return option.

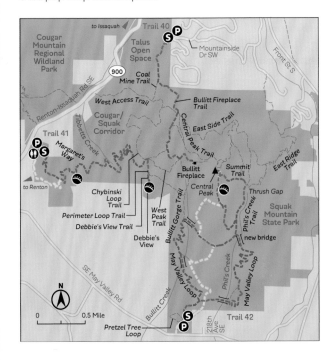

For a longer loop return, pick up the West Peak Trail from the Bullitt Gorge Trail junction and take this 0.4-mile rough path up and over the two wooded summits of the West Peak. The trail is steep and will give you a workout. You'll pass the collapsed remains of an old structure. The trail terminates at the Chybinski Loop Trail, 0.2 mile west of its junction with the Bullitt Fireplace Trail.

Now follow the lightly hiked Chybinski Loop Trail left. Pass Margaret's Way Trail (see Trail 41) and reach the West Access Trail in 1.2 miles. Then head left 0.1 mile to a junction with the Coal Mine Trail above a creek cascading through a gorge. Turn right here and reach the Bullitt Fireplace Trail in 0.2 mile.

41 Margaret's Way and Debbie's View

DISTANCE:	7 miles roundtrip
ELEVATION GAIN:	1600 feet
HIGH POINT:	1800 feet
DIFFICULTY:	Difficult
FITNESS:	Hikers, runners
FAMILY-FRIENDLY:	Yes—older children
DOG-FRIENDLY:	On leash
AMENITIES:	Restroom, picnic table
CONTACT/MAPS:	King County Parks; Green Trails Cougar Mountain/ Squak Mountain No. 203S
GPS:	N 47°30.469', W 122°05.270'

GETTING THERE

Driving: From Bellevue, follow I-405 south to I-90 and then head east, taking exit 15 in Issaquah. Turn right (south) onto State Route 900 (17th Avenue NW) and proceed for 3.3 miles. Then turn left into the Cougar/Squak Corridor and drive 0.1 mile to the trailhead and parking.

Mount Rainier from Debbie's View

From Renton, follow I-405 north to exit 5. Turn right and drive SR 900 (NE Park Drive, which becomes NE Sunset Boulevard) for 6.1 miles. Then turn right into the Cougar/Squak Corridor and drive 0.1 mile to the trailhead and parking.

Transit: King County Metro Trailhead Direct shuttle (seasonal)

Built in 2015 on land that was slated to be clear-cut, Margaret's Way winds its way up steep slopes through groves of mature trees. Not only will you get a good workout following this well-built and well-designed trail—you'll also earn some visual rewards. On a mountain known for its lack of views, you'll be granted two superb ones on this route—one that includes Mount Rainier.

GET MOVING

The trail starts in the old Issaquah Highlands Recreational Club—a sprawling RV park and campground on the west slope of Squak Mountain. The club closed and was sold to a logging company in 2012. The Issaquah Alps Trails Club, however, launched a campaign to save this 226-acre parcel. Through help from The Trust for Public Land, King County Parks was able to purchase it for $5 million. The park agency then added this large, forested tract housing the headwaters of Tibbets Creek to the Cougar/Squak Corridor, bringing its total to more than 700 acres—and connecting these two Issaquah Alps.

The trail was named for Issaquah City Parks planner Margaret Macleod, who died of cancer in 2013. Begin your hike up the old campground road, immediately passing the old clubhouse. Follow the steep road winding up forested slopes, passing old campsites. The way—always signed—diverts off the road a couple of times to follow new tread and take a more direct approach. At 0.6 mile, the trail leaves the campground complex for good.

Now in young forest, ignore side trails on your right. At 0.8 mile the trail intersects with an old road. Follow it left. The old road soon ends and true trail resumes, coming to a viewpoint over the May Creek Valley. It's a decent view, albeit limited—so push on, coming to a junction at 1.1 miles. Take it right 0.1 mile, coming to a bench at the edge of a forested opening (elev. 1110 feet) with a superb sweeping view of landscapes south and west. Lake Washington is visible—but not the Seattle skyline, as it is blocked by Cougar Mountain. Retrace your steps back to the main trail and continue right.

The trail now enters attractive mature timber and begins descending to a gap. The way then passes through a forest of big hemlocks and cedars above a ravine. At 1.7 miles from the trailhead, reach an unbridged crossing of Tibbets Creek (elev. 980 feet). The way then follows an old skid road and climbs along the northern edge of the ravine. It then crosses a small creek and negotiates some ledges in a hemlock forest before climbing in earnest via a series of short switchbacks.

At 3.1 miles reach a junction (elev. 1800 feet) with the Chybinski Loop Trail. Head right and soon come to a junction with the Perimeter Loop Trail. Take this trail right, ignoring the West Peak Trail left (which climbs Squak's viewless 1995-foot West Peak), and at 3.3 miles come to a junction. Take the spur right, following it 0.1 mile for a short descent to Debbie's View (elev. 1700 feet). Now enjoy the view south to Mount Rainier. Despite the fact that the massive Cedar Hills Regional Landfill is just below, this view doesn't stink at all!

GO FARTHER

For a little variation on the return and 500 feet or so of extra vertical climbing, from the Debbie's View spur junction, continue east on the Perimeter Loop Trail, reaching the Bullitt Gorge Trail in 0.4 mile. Then turn left and steeply climb 0.3 mile to a junction with the West Peak Trail. Turn left and steeply climb up and over the twin forested peaks of this summit, returning to the Perimeter Loop Trail near the Chybinski Loop in 0.4 mile. Then head back down Margaret's Way.

42 May Valley Loop

DISTANCE:	7.2 miles roundtrip
ELEVATION GAIN:	1900 feet
HIGH POINT:	2024 feet
DIFFICULTY:	Difficult
FITNESS:	Hikers, runners
FAMILY-FRIENDLY:	Yes
DOG-FRIENDLY:	On leash
AMENITIES:	Picnic tables, privy
CONTACT/MAPS:	Washington State Parks; Green Trails Cougar Mountain/Squak Mountain No. 203S
BEFORE YOU GO:	Discover Pass required. Parks open winter 8:00 AM to dusk, summer 6:30 AM to dusk.
GPS:	N 47°28.877', W 122°03.271'

GETTING THERE

Driving: From Bellevue, follow I-405 south to I-90 and then head east, taking exit 15 in Issaquah. Turn right (south) onto State Route 900 (17th Avenue NW) and proceed for 4.1 miles. Then turn left onto SE May Valley Road and continue for 2.5 miles. Turn left into Squak Mountain State Park and proceed to the parking area and trailhead.

From Renton, follow I-405 north to exit 5. Turn right and drive SR 900 (NE Park Drive, which becomes NE Sunset Boulevard) for 5.3 miles. Then turn right onto SE May Valley Road and continue for 2.5 miles. Turn left into Squak Mountain State Park and proceed to the parking area and trailhead.

Cascading creeks and the slew of bridges that span them are what this delightful loop is all about. Explore the south slopes of Squak Mountain, traversing mature forest groves and probing lush ravines. The May Valley Loop offers a great workout on wonderfully built and maintained trails that are never crowded.

GET MOVING

While the May Valley Loop Trail is open to horses, you probably won't see too many of them or anyone else on it. Come on a weekday and you might see no one! From the parking area, the trail heads north and soon comes to a gravel access road for the cluster of towers on the summit. It is gated just beyond two homes to the right—and makes for a good hike or run. Just across the gravel road is the trailhead for the Pretzel Tree Loop Trail (see Go Farther) and the continuation of the May Valley Loop.

The trail starts working its way upward. At 0.5 mile come to a junction where the loop actually begins. You'll be returning on the left—so carry on right. Cross the service road and gently descend, coming to a big bridge spanning Phil's Creek in a ravine shaded by big firs. The way then begins to climb

Bridge over Phil's Creek

once again. Pass a trail leading left that reconnects with the loop in 0.4 mile and ignore primitive side trails leading right. At 1.2 miles, bear right at a junction and continue across ferny slopes.

You are now on fairly new tread. The original trail here washed out a few years back. The new trail climbs farther away from the unstable slopes of the ravine and utilizes some wide switchbacks for an easy ascent. Pass a big ferny outcropping. At 2.4 miles, reach a junction (elev. 1200 feet) just after crossing Phil's Creek on a big, sturdy new bridge. To do the long loop, including ascending Squak's Central Peak, bear right. You'll be returning to this spot. If you want a shorter loop, head left (description later in text).

Now heading right, travel along Phil's Creek. At 2.6 miles come to a junction. The May Valley Loop Trail continues left. You will be returning on it, so head right now on the pedestrian-only Phil's Creek Trail. Enjoy a gentle climb above Phil's Creek to Thrush Gap, where at 3 miles the East Ridge Trail (see Trail 43) comes in from the right—and a little farther the Summit Trail leaves to the left. Take the Summit Trail, steeply climbing and reaching the service road in 3.3 miles. Now walk the road 0.1 mile right to the pretty much viewless and towered Central Peak, the summit of Squak (elev. 2024 feet). Then start heading down the road, passing the Summit Trail. Do look for a small side trail leading to a viewpoint—and if the weather is clear, check it out.

At 3.8 miles (0.4 mile from the summit), leave the road left for the May Valley Loop Trail. Quickly descend through big trees, coming to a familiar junction with the Phil's Creek Trail at 4.4 miles. Turn right and stay right at another familiar junction at 4.6 miles. Then continue on the May Valley Loop, crossing a creek at the head of a ravine and coming to the south access road (elev. 1050 feet) at 4.9 miles.

Now turn right and walk the road, gaining elevation. At 5.1 miles, leave the road left for the continuation of the May Valley Loop Trail. Continue climbing before crossing Bullitt Creek and coming to a junction (elev. 1275 feet) at 5.3 miles. Here the Bullitt Gorge Trail travels right 0.7 mile to the Bullitt Fireplace Trail (see Trail 40). Go left, descending with the help of switchbacks in attractive mature forest. Bullitt Creek tumbles out of view in a nearby ravine. Stay left where a trail leads right to a housing development and soon cross Bullitt Creek on a bridge.

At 6 miles, come to a junction where a short trail leads left to the south access road. Stay right and continue to descend, reaching a familiar junction where the loop begins at 6.7 miles. Now head right, retracing familiar ground and returning to your start at 7.2 miles.

GO FARTHER

Definitely take the time—especially if you have young hikers with you—to walk the 0.3-mile Pretzel Tree Loop Trail. It's a story panel trail about a deer mouse looking for a fabled pretzel tree. See if you can find it with him.

43 East Ridge

DISTANCE:	8 miles roundtrip
ELEVATION GAIN:	2000 feet
HIGH POINT:	2024 feet
DIFFICULTY:	Difficult
FITNESS:	Hikers, runners
FAMILY-FRIENDLY:	Yes
DOG-FRIENDLY:	On leash
AMENITIES:	Restrooms at Community Center Park
CONTACT/MAPS:	King County Parks; Green Trails Cougar Mountain/ Squak Mountain No. 203S
GPS:	N 47°31.642', W 122°02.034'

GETTING THERE

Driving: From Bellevue, follow I-405 south to I-90 and then head east, taking exit 17 in Issaquah. Turn right (south) onto Front Street and proceed for 0.8 mile, turning left onto SE Bush Street (two blocks south of the Sunset Way intersection). Continue for two blocks to the "little yellow house" and parking. Parking is also available at the Issaquah Community Center on south side of SE Bush Street.

   Transit: King County Metro lines 200, 208, 554

One of the longest and more challenging routes to Squak Mountain's 2024-foot summit, the East Ridge is also the most varied route and the least traveled. An added bonus is starting right from Issaquah, walking paved paths and greenway en route to the state park. This hike offers a real town and country flavor with exceptional après-hike options in the form of cafés, brewpubs, and restaurants at trail's end. There are big trees, lush ravines, and some views of nearby Tiger Mountain too.

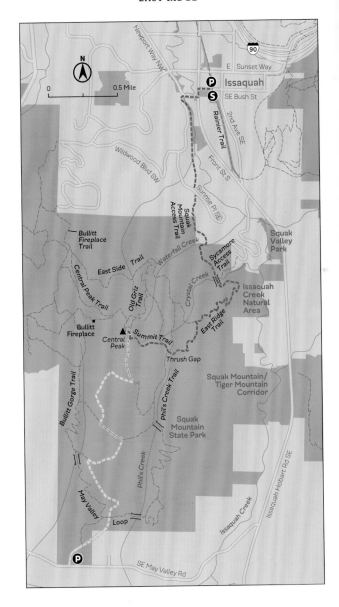

Vine maple jungle along East Ridge Trail

GET MOVING

Start your adventure from the Issaquah Trail Center a.k.a. the little yellow house. It's the headquarters of the Issaquah Alps Trails Club, which is responsible for much of the public land surrounding this sprawling suburb. Be sure to stop at the kiosk and read about the club's founder, Harvey Manning (see sidebar "Cougar Mountain's Curmudgeonly Conservationist"), one of the greatest champions of trails and wild places this state has ever seen.

The paved Rainier Trail (see Trail 30) runs north–south past the house. But for this trip, you want to walk west on SE Bush Street for two blocks to Front Street S. Then walk one block south and head west onto Newport Way SW, crossing Issaquah Creek. At 0.25 mile, turn left (south) onto Wildwood Boulevard SW and immediately come to the Squak

Mountain Access Trail on your left. Take it, following alongside Issaquah Creek and coming to a small dam. Then continue through some housing complexes, following signs for "Squak Mountain Access Trail." (Note: this section of the trail may be closed to the public—if so, walk Wildwood Boulevard SW to Sunrise Place SW and pick up the trail again.)

At 1 mile, cross Sunrise Place SW and leave the urban landscape behind. Begin traversing forested slopes, passing some big trees, and steeply ascend with the help of steps. Then descend into a ravine to cross Waterfall Creek, and at 1.9 miles reach a junction with the Sycamore Access Trail. This junction, like most on the mountain, is well signed. Now continue right onto the East Ridge Trail and soon cross Crystal Creek on a bridge. Then begin steeply climbing—thankfully via switchbacks—up a forested rib draped in salal and Oregon grape. Gaps in the forest canopy allow sneak peeks at Tiger Mountain's Poo Poo Point across the valley. At 3.3 miles, reach a junction with the lightly traveled East Side Trail.

Bear left, remaining on the East Ridge Trail, and reach a junction with Phil's Creek Trail just beyond Thrush Gap at 3.6 miles. The way left leads 0.4 mile to the May Valley Loop (see Trail 42). You want to head right, soon coming to another junction. Phil's Creek Trail continues north 0.6 mile to meet up with the East Ridge Trail. You want to go left on the Summit Trail, reaching a service road after a short, steep, 0.3-mile climb. Then turn right onto a gravel service road and reach the multi-towered, 2024-foot Central Peak summit in 0.1 mile. The views from Squak's highest point aren't much, if any at all, but be satisfied that you've burned some calories and enjoyed some quiet trails! Consider the following options below to extend your hike or run.

GO FARTHER
You can make a couple of loops on Squak's summits before heading back down the East Ridge Trail to return to your start.

Consider the Old Griz Trail, which leaves from the summit and heads northeast, connecting with Phil's Creek Trail in 0.4 mile. Then continue north on Phil's Creek Trail, reaching the East Side Trail in another 0.3 mile. Now head right on the East Side Trail, traversing steep slopes and lush, creek-fed ravines, passing mossy boulders, and dropping and climbing a little to reach the East Ridge Trail in 0.9 mile. From here, it's 3.3 miles left back to your start.

You can also combine with a trip to the Bullitt Fireplace (see Trail 40) by heading north on the Central Peak Trail 0.3 mile and then left on the Bullitt Fireplace Trail for another 0.3 mile. Follow the Bullitt Fireplace Trail north for 0.8 mile to its junction with the East Side Trail. Then head right 1.7 miles on the East Side Trail—which starts as an old skid road before transitioning to single track—back to the East Ridge Trail.

ISSAQUAH ALPS: TIGER MOUNTAIN

44 Tradition Lake Plateau

DISTANCE:	More than 8 miles of trails
ELEVATION GAIN:	Up to 250 feet
HIGH POINT:	660 feet
DIFFICULTY:	Easy to moderate
FITNESS:	Hikers, runners, walkers
FAMILY-FRIENDLY:	Yes, partial wheelchair- and stroller-friendly
DOG-FRIENDLY:	On leash
AMENITIES:	Privies, picnic tables, benches, interpretive signs
CONTACT/MAPS:	Washington DNR; Green Trails Tiger Mountain/Taylor Mountain No. 204S
BEFORE YOU GO:	Discover Pass required. Parking lot fills fast on weekends, requiring street parking (permissible and no pass required, but be sure you are well off-road and adhere to any no parking signs).
GPS:	N 47°31.779', W 121°59.745'

GETTING THERE

Driving: From Bellevue, follow I-405 south to I-90 and then head east, taking exit 20 (High Point). Turn right (south) onto 270th Avenue SE, and then immediately turn right onto SE 79th Street. Proceed 0.8 mile to the High Point Trailhead and parking.

Transit: King County Metro line 208 stops at 270th Avenue SE; Trailhead Direct shuttle (seasonal) stops at the East Sunset Way Trailhead.

Take to an array of easy trails traversing a wooded plateau at the foot of West Tiger Mountain. Tradition Lake's trails can be enjoyed by hikers, runners, and walkers of all ages and abilities. And while this semi-wild corner of the sprawling Tiger Mountain State Forest abuts Issaquah and is extremely popular, there is plenty of room to roam. Enjoy plenty of surprises—including some solitude and serenity.

GET MOVING

There are more than 8 miles of trails within the Tradition Lake Plateau, allowing for numerous loops of varying distances. The area is perfect for an after-work run or an all-day hike. While the main approach is via the High Point Trailhead, the plateau can also easily be accessed right from Issaquah from trailheads off East Sunset Way and the High School Trail. The trails within the Department of Natural Resources's (DNR) ownership are well marked. The trails within the City of Issaquah's ownership, however, are not marked as well. Be sure to have a map with you, so you don't end up where you don't want to be.

Tradition Lake became a Natural Resources Conservation Area (NRCA) in 1994, thanks to the Issaquah City Council. These enlightened city officials wanted to have the city's preserved lands managed in accordance with the abutting NRCA. While this parcel is traversed by powerlines and a gas

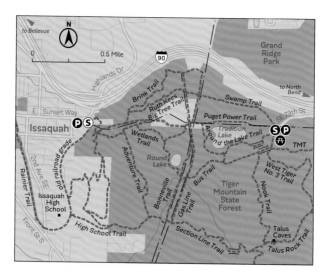

line, it also contains a couple of high-quality kettle ponds, extensive wetlands, mature forest, and some old-growth trees as well.

The nearly level 1.5-mile Around the Lake Trail is one popular route; its first 0.5 mile is ADA accessible. There are also interpretive signs and animal track plates along the way. The Around the Lake Trail then skirts 16-acre Tradition Lake's west shoreline, passing a good lake viewpoint. It then connects with the Puget Power Trail (service road), continuing east past another viewpoint before returning to the trailhead. A couple of creeks feed into this tranquil lake, but it has no outlet. Water seeps through the gravel bottom to a series of springs.

The Bus Trail is another popular plateau trail. The first 0.5 mile of this trail is also ADA accessible and nearly level. There is a short connector with the Around the Lake Trail, allowing for an ADA-accessible loop of more than 1 mile. The key attraction on this trail is the hull of an old bus, lying on its side and being reclaimed by the forest. The old bus, believed to be a model from the 1930s, was once used by logging companies to transport workers on the mountain. It was abandoned here in the early 1950s. The Bus Trail continues west another 0.3 mile, connecting with the Gas Line, Bonneville, and Wetlands Trails.

The Wetlands Trail is the most interesting of the lot. This 0.5-mile trail, lined with split-rail fencing in spots, skirts the 2-acre Round Lake and traverses wetlands where Oregon ashes grow. It terminates at the Puget Power Trail, which can be followed 1 mile east back to the parking lot. The nearby lightly hiked, 0.8-mile Adventure Trail can be taken for a longer loop. This trail traverses tall timber and climbs a 660-foot knoll. It connects to the High School Trail, which leads west 0.7 mile to the old railroad grade, past Issaquah High School, and on to the Rainier Trail (see Trail 30).

The Swamp Trail is enjoyable for children. It's an easy path following the adventures of Zoe the raccoon through a series

Tradition Lake

of panels. Children will learn about the swamp through Zoe and her wild friends. The trail ends in 0.7 mile, where you can continue on the Ruth Kees Big Tree Trail for 0.5 mile. Named for a local conservationist, this trail actually is swampier than the Swamp Trail. Its biggest draw, however, is its big trees, including one gigantic Douglas fir, the largest and oldest on Tiger Mountain. You can return to the trailhead via the 1.1-mile Puget Power Trail or the 0.7-mile Brink Trail back to the Swamp Trail. The Brink Trail runs along the edge of the plateau above the East Fork Issaquah Creek valley containing I-90. The roar of the highway will remind you that it is just below.

The Puget Power Trail ends at the west edge of the plateau, where there is a good view over Issaquah and out to Cougar Mountain. From here, some unmarked trails lead south, and a well-constructed and steep-in-places trail heads west, descending 300 feet to the East Sunset Way Trailhead.

45 | West Tiger Mountain

DISTANCE:	Up to 7.8 miles roundtrip
ELEVATION GAIN:	Up to 2850 feet
HIGH POINT:	2948 feet
DIFFICULTY:	Difficult
FITNESS:	Hikers
FAMILY-FRIENDLY:	Yes
DOG-FRIENDLY:	On leash
AMENITIES:	Privies, picnic tables, benches, interpretive signs
CONTACT/MAPS:	Washington DNR; Green Trails Tiger Mountain/Taylor Mountain No. 204S
BEFORE YOU GO:	Discover Pass required. Parking lot fills fast on weekends, requiring street parking (permissible and no pass required, but be sure you are well off-road and adhere to any no parking signs).
GPS:	N 47°31.779', W 121°59.745'

View of Mount Si and neighboring peaks

GETTING THERE

Driving: From Bellevue, follow I-405 south to I-90 and then head east, taking exit 20 (High Point). Turn right (south) onto 270th Avenue SE and then immediately turn right onto SE 79th Street. Proceed 0.8 mile to High Point Trailhead and parking.

   Transit: King County Metro line 208 stops at 270th Avenue SE.

A popular peak ascended year round by budding hikers (and experienced hikers conditioning for bigger mountains), West Tiger offers a great workout to all. The mountain has three summits, although most folks stop at West Tiger No. 3 with its limited views. But if you have the energy to push on, do so—West Tiger No. 1 boasts wide-reaching views from Mount Rainier to the Seattle skyline against a backdrop of snow-capped Olympic Mountains.

GET MOVING

Several trails diverge from the busy High Point Trailhead. Follow signs for the West Tiger No. 3 Trail. Immediately bear

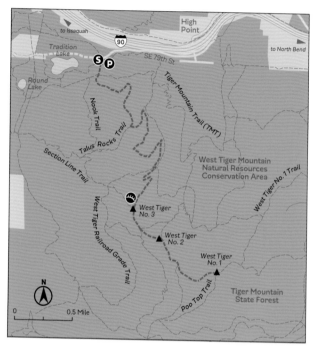

left at the Around the Lake Trail junction. Shortly afterward, bear left again at the Bus Trail junction, and then continue right at the next junction with the Tiger Mountain Trail (see Trail 46).

The trail wastes no time climbing, following old skid roads transformed into a wide trail. The tread is generally good, but there are some rocky and steep sections interspersed between smooth and moderately graded trail. At 0.9 mile, just after crossing a small creek, bear left at the Talus Rocks Trail junction (elev. 1140 feet). Shortly afterward, ignore a side trail left leading to the primitive Cable Line path.

Notice the abrupt transition from deciduous forest cover to stately conifers. At 1.9 miles reach an unmarked junction with the West Tiger Railroad Grade Trail (elev. 1980 feet). Continue straight, heading up a series of tight, steep switchbacks. Cross the primitive Cable Line path (an unofficial, unmaintained trail often used by hikers for extreme conditioning), reaching a couple of good viewpoints east to Mount Si and the Cascade Front and south to the towered summit of West Tiger No. 2. At 2.7 miles reach the 2522-foot summit of West Tiger No. 3. Once upon a time the view from this spot was superb. But no longer—now formerly cutover forest has reclaimed this knob. You'll have to be content with a window view to Seattle and the Olympics—or continue farther and higher.

The trail descends via tight switchbacks about 80 feet, soon coming to the foundation of a long-gone fire lookout. Here through the salal is a decent view east. But be careful, as the drop-off is pronounced. The trail continues and steeply climbs, coming to a junction with the Tiger Mountain Trail (see Trail 46) at 2.9 miles.

Continue straight up a steep ridge, coming to a service road just below the towered 2757-foot summit of West Tiger No. 2 at 3.1 miles. The view here too has long succumbed to greenery. Continue hiking on the service road, descending 250 feet to a gated junction at 3.4 miles. Bear left, steeply climb, and at 3.7 miles reach another gate and the Hiker's Hut (elev. 2800 feet), resembling a space capsule. Enjoy excellent views here of Mount Rainier to the south and Squak, Cougar, Seattle, Puget Sound, and the Olympics to the west.

If you're compelled to bag West Tiger No. 1, follow the Bypass Trail left through thick, dark timber, skirting below a bevy of towers (closed and dangerous to enter) to a junction. Then head right for a short, steep ascent on the Poo Top Trail, reaching a gate at 3.9 miles, just below the 2948-foot summit. Return the way you came, or consider the following options.

GO FARTHER

For a quiet lollipop loop, follow the Poo Top Trail to the Hidden Forest Trail 0.9 mile down a steep ridge to the Tiger Mountain

Trail (TMT). Then head right 1.4 miles back to the West Tiger No. 3 Trail. From West Tiger No. 3, you can descend (better to ascend) on the brutally steep Section Line Trail 0.9 mile to a junction. Here you can continue left on a better section of the Section Line Trail, coming to the Gas Line and Bonneville Trails in 0.8 mile, which can be followed north to the Bus Trail for a return to the trailhead.

From the junction midway on the Section Line Trail, you can also head right and descend on the pleasant 0.7-mile Nook Trail to the Bus Trail—or continue east on the 0.4-mile Talus Rocks Trail back to West Tiger No. 3 Trail. Set among big trees, the Talus Rocks are a collection of talus caves, some of the largest in the state. A small loop path squeezes through, around, and over some of the talus.

And there are a couple of lightly traveled trails that descend West Tiger No. 1, leading northeast to a trailhead on SE Preston Way. Don't forget your map.

46 Tiger Mountain Trail

DISTANCE:	16 miles one-way
ELEVATION GAIN:	2750 feet
HIGH POINT:	2550 feet
DIFFICULTY:	Difficult
FITNESS:	Hikers, runners
FAMILY-FRIENDLY:	Yes
DOG-FRIENDLY:	On leash
AMENITIES:	Restrooms, picnic tables
CONTACT/MAPS:	Washington DNR; Green Trails Tiger Mountain/Taylor Mountain No. 204S
BEFORE YOU GO:	Discover Pass required. High Point Trailhead parking lot fills fast on weekends, requiring street parking (permissible and no pass required, but be sure you are well off-road and adhere to no parking signs).
GPS:	N 47°31.779', W 121°59.745'

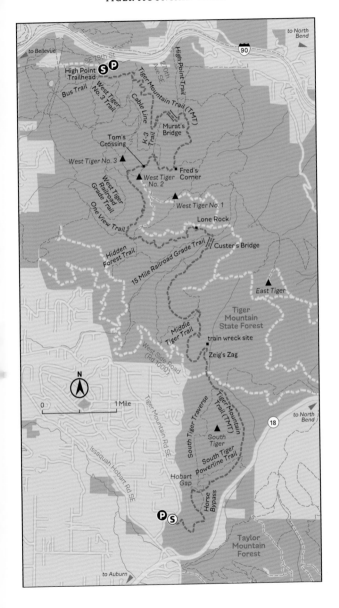

GETTING THERE

Driving: *North Trailhead:* From Bellevue, follow I-405 south to I-90 and then head east, taking exit 20 (High Point). Turn right (south) onto 270th Avenue SE and then immediately turn right onto SE 79th Street. Proceed 0.8 mile to High Point Trailhead and parking. *South Trailhead:* From Bellevue, follow I-405 south to I-90 and then head east, taking exit 17 in Issaquah. Turn right onto Front Street, which becomes the Issaquah Hobart Road SE (alternatively follow Newport Way NW to avoid downtown Issaquah congestion), and proceed for 8.2 miles. Then turn left (just before the State Route 18 interchange) onto Tiger Mountain Road SE and continue for 0.3 mile to the trailhead on your right. Park on the left side of the road.

    Transit: *North Trailhead:* King County Metro line 208 stops at 270th Avenue SE.

Hike or run across the sprawling Tiger Mountain State Forest from north to south on this grand 16-mile-long trail. While the distance may appear daunting to some, the elevation gain shouldn't be. After an initial 4-mile uphill grunt, the trail continues on a predominantly downhill trajectory. Skirt summits, round ravines, traverse mature forest, cross crashing creeks, and savor solitude along the way. Much of this well-built trail sees just a few people each week.

GET MOVING

This is a great trail for conditioning, solitude, and seeing the heart of Tiger Mountain State Forest. If you can't shuttle a vehicle to do the whole thing in one sweep—or it's a tad too much to tackle—consider shorter out-and-backs (or loops when combined with adjacent trails) from either end. The southern end sees far less use than the northern end. The three southernmost miles are also open to horses—but not bikes. This is one of the few bike-free trails in the southern half

Enveloping greenery along the Tiger Mountain Trail

of the forest. Following is a brief description of the trail from north to south. Several trails diverge from the High Point Trailhead. Follow signs for the West Tiger No. 3 Trail. Immediately bear left at the Around the Lake Trail junction. Shortly afterward, bear left again at the Bus Trail junction; then continue left at the next junction for the start of Tiger Mountain Trail (TMT). The well-built trail heads east across West Tiger's northern slopes, steadily ascending. At 0.8 mile it crosses the brutally steep Cable Line primitive path. It then swings south, switchbacks, and levels for a bit. In a lush undergrowth of ferns, vine maples, and devil's club, come to a big bridge spanning a creek. Soon afterward cross another bridge.

The trail then passes the lightly hiked K-3 Trail and descends 300 feet, coming to an engineering wonder on the trail, Murat's Bridge (elev. 1400 feet), at 2.7 miles. Named in honor of avid young outdoorsman Murat Danishek—who died at the age of thirty-two due to heart conditions—the high, 200-foot-long bridge spanning High Point Creek was funded by his parents. The way then passes the High Point Trail (elev. 1100 feet) and shortly afterward the Lingering Trail, at 2.9 miles.

The TMT resumes, steadily climbing. Cross a couple of small creeks en route, reaching Fred's Corner (elev. 1850 feet) at 3.8 miles. Here a section of the West Tiger Railroad Grade Trail heads left. You want to continue right, climbing. Round a ravine and cross High Point Creek via a bridge once again before reaching a junction (elev. 2200 feet) at 4.5 miles. Here K-3 and the West Tiger Railroad Grade depart right.

Continue left, passing a view east to Mount Si, and at 5.2 miles come to Tom's Crossing (elev. 2550 feet), the highest point on the trail. Here a trail steeply climbs left to the towered, no-view summit of West Tiger No. 2. The TMT skirts the summit on new tread, traversing towering timber and crossing the popular West Tiger No. 3 Trail (elev. 2475 feet) at 5.5 miles. Soon afterward, pass the Seattle View Trail and then begin a long traverse of West Tiger's western slopes, slowly descending and passing window views west to Puget Sound.

At 7 miles come to a junction with the One View Trail. Soon afterward, cross the Hidden Forest Trail. The TMT then swings east, traversing West Tiger's southern slopes and continuing a generally gentle descent. Pass more creeks, views of East Tiger Mountain, more named trail spots, and a big erratic known as Lone Rock near the halfway point on the trail. At 8.7 miles cross the 15 Mile Railroad Grade Trail and then descend on new tread to Custer's Bridge spanning Fifteenmile Creek (elev. 1950 feet).

The TMT then once again swings south, traversing Middle Tiger Mountain's western slopes. Skirt a recent cut and travel through groves of mature firs. Cross a couple more creeks too. A few short, uphill sections break the downhill momentum. At 10.7 miles cross the Middle Tiger Trail. The trail then continues descending, following an old railroad grade and swinging around a small knob. It crosses a logging road and then reaches a switchback known as Zeig's Zag near the site of train-wreck ruins. At 12.3 miles reach the West Side Road (Road 1000). Now follow a gated road south for a short distance, passing the South Tiger Traverse on your right. Shortly afterward, trail tread resumes.

The TMT now swings east of South Tiger Mountain, coming to a powerline swath (elev. 1300 feet) at 13.6 miles. Follow the powerline service road right for a short distance and pick up the trail again, heading south. The trail then heads into cool forest and crosses a creek in a small notch known as Hobart Gap at 14.5 miles. Here the South Tiger Traverse heads north, and the Horse Bypass heads south. Stay on the TMT, traveling through some big trees before reaching the South Trailhead (elev. 550 feet) at 16 miles.

47 Poo Poo Point

DISTANCE:	Chirico: 3.8 miles roundtrip; Poo Poo Point: 9 miles roundtrip
ELEVATION GAIN:	Chirico: 1650 feet; Poo Poo Point: 1900 feet
HIGH POINT:	Chirico: 1825 feet; Poo Poo Point: 1900 feet
DIFFICULTY:	Difficult
FITNESS:	Runners, hikers
FAMILY-FRIENDLY:	Yes
DOG-FRIENDLY:	On leash
AMENITIES:	Privies, picnic tables, benches
CONTACT/MAPS:	Washington DNR; Green Trails Tiger Mountain/Taylor Mountain No. 204S
BEFORE YOU GO:	Discover Pass required at High Point Trailhead. Chirico Trail parking lot fills fast. No parking (tow zone) on Issaquah Hobart Road, but there is a private (pay) lot nearby just north of trailhead.
GPS:	N 47°29.801', W 122°01.307'

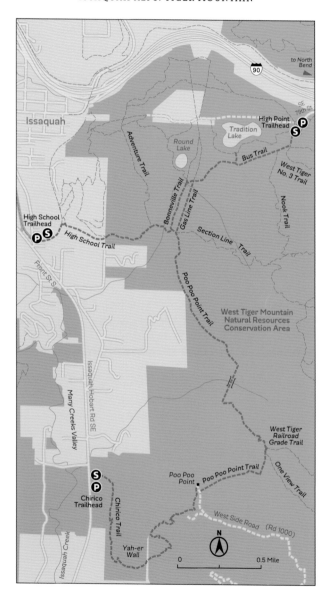

GETTING THERE

Driving: *Chirico Trailhead:* From Bellevue, follow I-405 south to I-90 and then head east, taking exit 17 in Issaquah. Turn right onto Front Streets, which becomes Issaquah Hobart Road SE (alternatively follow Newport Way NW to avoid downtown Issaquah congestion), and proceed for 3 miles to the trailhead on your left. *High School Trailhead:* From Bellevue, follow I-405 south to I-90 and then head east, taking exit 17 in Issaquah. Turn right (south) onto Front Street S. (Alternatively follow Newport Way NW to avoid downtown Issaquah congestion), and proceed for 1.6 miles. Then turn left onto 2nd Avenue SE, and after 200 hundred feet come to the trailhead on your right. *High Point Trailhead:* From Bellevue, follow I-405 south to I-90 and then head east, taking exit 20 (High Point). Turn right (south) onto 270th Avenue SE and then immediately turn right onto SE 79th Street. Proceed 0.8 mile to High Point Trailhead and parking.

Transit: *Chirico Trailhead:* King County Metro Trailhead Direct shuttle (seasonal). *High School Trailhead:* King County Metro Trailhead Direct shuttle (seasonal). *High Point Trailhead:* King County Metro line 208 stops at 270th Avenue SE.

Nothing stinks about Poo Poo Point, the best viewpoint on Tiger Mountain. From this high, open, grassy spot revered by paragliders, stare out at Squak Mountain, Cougar Mountain, Issaquah, Lake Sammamish, and the Bellevue skyline. There's a view southwest too, a pretty darned good one of Mount Rainier. The point is extremely popular—one of the busiest trails in the state. But it's no walk in the park—you'll have to earn those views.

GET MOVING

There are two main approaches to Poo Poo Point. Choose between the direct, waste-no-time-getting-there Chirico Trail and the longer Poo Poo Point Trail, which traverses the Many

Paraglider taking off from Poo Poo Point

Creeks Valley and quiet, mature forest. In addition to having a gentler grade, the latter trail also sees significantly less people. Shuttle a car and head up one and out the other.

CHIRICO TRAIL

Start by walking across a field used by paragliders to touch down. Do look up and be alert as you traverse this spot. This trail is named for the owner of the abutting Seattle Para-gliding company, who worked hard with his employees, other volunteers, and Department of Natural Resources (DNR) offi-cials to create this trail and top-notch paragliding facilities at Tiger Mountain.

Once past the field, a wooden bear and patriotic arch greet you. Pass through the arch and begin to climb. The way is steep and means business. Elaborate stone steps help with the ascent and with elevating your heart rate. The trail heads south to avoid the steep face of Yah-er Wall. It then swings east, still climbing in earnest. The path then heads north, still on a hell-bent course to gain elevation. At 1.6 miles emerge at the grassy, open South Viewpoint Landing. If the weather is favorable, expect to be blown away with a wonderful Mount Rainier view.

Then continue a little farther, coming to the closed-to-vehicles West Side Road. Walk this road a short distance left and come to the North Launch Viewpoint (picnic tables and privy) on Poo Poo Point (elev. 1850 feet) at 1.8 miles. Sit for a while on what once was a stump field. Stare out over Issaquah all the way to Mount Baker if it's clear. Squak and Cougar Mountains should be in view—as well as paragliders in various stages of takeoff and flight.

POO POO POINT TRAIL

The longer, classic way to reach panoramic Poo Poo Point is via this trail, reached from either the High School Trail or High Point Trailhead. For the High School approach, follow the old railroad grade for 0.3 mile, coming to the High School Trail near Issaquah High School. Then follow this old road, moderately climbing, passing some unmarked trails and the Adventure Trail, and reaching a junction (elev. 500 feet) in a powerline and gas line swath at 1.2 miles.

If you're starting from High Point, follow the Bus Trail west for 0.9 mile to the Gas Line Trail. Then take this path 0.3 mile south to a junction. The distance is the same as the High School Trail—and without the 350-foot vertical climb.

Now follow the Poo Poo Point Trail (seasonally open to horses) south. Utilizing an old logging road, this trail readily gains elevation at first before easing up. Hike through cedar groves and mossy, ferny forest. Enter the Many Creeks Valley. You'll actually only be crossing a few, as these creeks' many tributaries feed into them above. There's a couple of bridge crossings, including an impressive one over a creek tumbling down a ravine.

The old logging road peters out and the trail takes a much steeper route up a knoll adorned in big trees. At 4 miles reach a junction (elev. 1900 feet). Here the One View Trail continues upward to the Tiger Mountain Trail, and the West Tiger Railroad Grade (see Trail 48) heads left and right. You want to go right on it, soon leaving the grade and steeply dropping 125 feet to an old road bed. Cross a creek and follow this road-now-trail, reaching Poo Poo Point at 4.5 miles.

And the Poo Poo? It's a reference to the sound made by steam whistles during logging operations. It once was a common sound in these parts, now replaced by the cheers of jubilant paragliders, hikers, and trail runners.

48 West Tiger Railroad Grade

DISTANCE:	7.2 miles roundtrip
ELEVATION GAIN:	Up to 1600 feet
HIGH POINT:	2000 feet
DIFFICULTY:	Moderate
FITNESS:	Hikers, runners
FAMILY-FRIENDLY:	Yes
DOG-FRIENDLY:	On leash
AMENITIES:	Privies, picnic tables, benches, interpretive signs
CONTACT/MAPS:	Washington DNR; Green Trails Tiger Mountain/Taylor Mountain No. 204S
BEFORE YOU GO:	Discover Pass required. Parking lot fills fast on weekends, requiring street parking (permissible and no pass required, but be sure you are well off-road and adhere to any no parking signs).
GPS:	N 47°31.779', W 121°59.745'

GETTING THERE

Driving: From Bellevue, follow I-405 south to I-90 and then head east, taking exit 20 (High Point). Turn right (south) onto 270th Avenue SE and then immediately turn right onto SE 79th Street. Proceed 0.8 mile to the High Point Trailhead and parking.

Mature timber along the West Tiger Railroad Grade

Transit: King County Metro line 208 stops at 270th Avenue SE.

One of the easiest trails within Tiger Mountain State Forest, the West Tiger Railroad Grade is also one of the quietest. Attribute the quiet to the fact that you must steeply hike a couple of miles to reach this trail. But once there, you can hike more than 3 near-level, near-deserted miles on an old logging railroad bed that wraps around the northern reaches of West Tiger Mountain. There are a handful of old railroad artifacts strewn about too—so keep a trained eye out for them.

GET MOVING

The West Tiger Railroad Grade Trail runs for more than 3 miles at an elevation hovering between 1900 and 2000 feet. It can be accessed from several trails to create loops of various distances. The one described here, utilizing the West Tiger No. 3 and Poo Poo Point Trails, makes for a good day hike.

Starting from the busy High Point Trailhead, follow signs for the West Tiger No. 3 Trail. Immediately bear left at the Around the Lake Trail junction. Shortly afterward, bear left again at the Bus Trail junction (you'll be returning on this trail), and then continue right at the next junction with the Tiger Mountain Trail.

Now start climbing. At 0.9 mile, just after crossing a small creek, bear left at the Talus Rocks Trail junction. Shortly afterward, ignore a side trail left leading to the primitive Cable Line path. At 1.9 miles reach an unmarked junction with the West Tiger Railroad Grade Trail (elev. 1980 feet). Head right and immediately notice the lack of fellow hikers—they're all heading for West Tiger.

A remnant from the old railroad (which ceased operations in the 1920s), the grade cuts through a mainly deciduous forest—the big conifers long logged off. The forest and terrain look very much like they belong to the Appalachian Mountains. During the winter months, when the foliage is bare, you can catch glimpses of the valleys below and hills beyond. At 2.4 miles come to the Section Line Trail—a brutally steep path that may be used to shorten your loop (and the life of your knees).

The West Tiger Railroad Grade continues on a fairly easy course, coming to the unmarked and lightly hiked Seattle View Trail at 2.7 miles. The trail now swings around a bowl above Many Creeks Valley. The way gets rougher too, with some trail slumping and minor ups and downs, especially at some of the creek crossings that once were spanned by

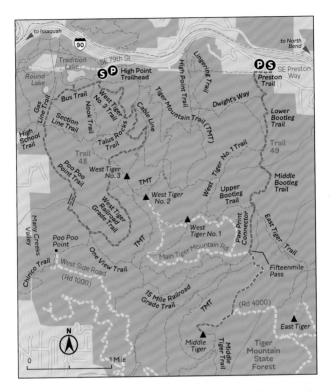

trestles. Most of the crossings now are unbridged, but negotiating them shouldn't pose any problems.

Look for relics of the railroad along the way, including remaining rails. And do leave all remnants in place for others to enjoy. Pass beneath draping vine maples, which brighten the understory with golden hues come October. At 4 miles come to a stile and junction. The Railroad Grade Trail continues straight—leaving the original grade and ending at Poo Poo Point.

You want to head right on the Poo Poo Point Trail, at first steeply descending—then following a more moderate descent on an old logging roadbed. At 6 miles come to a junction with the Section Line Trail. Head left here, soon coming to another junction. Go right on the Gas Line Trail, and at 6.3 miles reach another junction. Head right here on the delightful Bus Trail, returning to your start at 7.2 miles.

And in case you're wondering why the railroad grade abruptly terminates on both ends—it's because the train cars were hoisted to and fro via a tram to a mill in High Point.

GO FARTHER

You can follow the West Tiger Railroad Grade left (east) from the West Tiger No. 3 Trail as well. The grade travels 1.4 miles before ending at High Point Creek. From here the trail continues as a steep path, climbing 0.2 mile to the Tiger Mountain Trail (TMT). Consider approaching the trail via the TMT and hiking the whole grade, exiting via the Poo Poo Point Trail. It's a journey of 11.3 miles.

49 Middle Tiger Mountain

DISTANCE:	10 miles roundtrip
ELEVATION GAIN:	Up to 2200 feet
HIGH POINT:	2607 feet
DIFFICULTY:	Difficult
FITNESS:	Hikers, runners
FAMILY-FRIENDLY:	Yes
DOG-FRIENDLY:	On leash
AMENITIES:	Privy, picnic tables
CONTACT/MAPS:	Washington DNR; Green Trails Tiger Mountain/Taylor Mountain No. 204S
GPS:	N 47°44.669', W 121°59.177'

GETTING THERE

Driving: From Bellevue, follow I-405 south to I-90 and then head east, taking exit 22. Turn right onto SE 82nd Street and then immediately turn right onto SE Preston Way. Proceed

0.5 mile to the trailhead on your left near a DOT facility. Park on the south side of the road away from the facility entrance.

West Tiger teems with hikers and trail runners, while East Tiger entertains brigades of mountain bikers. Middle Tiger Mountain, however, remains off the recreational radar. Hike or run to this sleeping tiger in the heart of the state forest with a good chance of having it all to yourself. Explore little-known trails and keep your senses tuned to the possibility of perhaps seeing a real tiger—that is, a bobcat or cougar—in this sprawling backyard wilderness.

GET MOVING

Middle Tiger can be reached from several approaches. The shortest (3.7 miles one-way) is from the Tiger Summit Trailhead—but to reach it, you'll first need to hike the open-to-bikes Iverson Railroad Trail to the Tiger Mountain Trail (TMT) to the Middle Tiger Mountain Trail. The route described here is

A hiker negotiates a steep section of the Lower Bootleg Trail.

far more interesting, taking you across the eastern half of the West Tiger Natural Resources Conservation Area, which sees a fraction of the hikers the western half sees.

Start by following the Preston Trail south through a patch of forest, soon coming to a powerline right-of-way. Follow this unattractive section right, eventually bending back into the forest at 0.6 mile. Now start climbing in mossy, mature woods, reaching a junction (elev. 980 feet) with Dwight's Way at 1.1 miles, which connects with the High Point and Lingering Trails. You want to go left on the Lower Bootleg Trail, steadily and at times steeply climbing, reaching a junction (elev. 1520 feet) with the West Tiger No. 1 Trail at 1.6 miles.

Continue straight for a short distance—then stay left where the West Tiger No. 1 Trail departs right, offering a quiet alternative route (and good workout) up that peak. Now on the Middle Bootleg Trail, traverse steep slopes, cross the East Fork of Issaquah Creek, and then climb more steadily. At 2.6 miles come to another junction. Here the Upper Bootleg Trail departs right for West Tiger No. 1. You want to stay left and then stay right at the next junction, where a trail takes off for East Tiger Mountain.

Now on the Paw Print Connector, begin a slight descent, coming to a short road spur leading to the Main Tiger Mountain Road (Road 4000) at Fifteenmile Pass (elev. 2100 feet) at 3.3 miles. Here find a picnic table and composting toilet. Across the road, the 15 Mile Railroad Grade Trail leads 0.2 mile to the TMT. You want to head left on the closed-to-public-vehicles road. It makes a gentle climb along a recent clear-cut, granting a great view of West Tiger Mountain. At 4.3 miles bear right onto a lightly used road and follow it, gently climbing to its end. Then locate a stile indicating the start of the Middle Tiger Mountain Trail. Follow it into thick timber for a short climb, topping out on the forested summit of 2607-foot Middle Tiger Mountain. Pretty anticlimactic, this hike is all about the journey and the excitement of going where few Tiger Mountain aficionados have gone before.

GO FARTHER

For a slightly longer return, continue on the Middle Tiger Mountain Trail, steeply dropping in tall timber and coming to the TMT in 0.3 mile. Then turn right on the TMT and follow it 1.9 miles to the 15 Mile Railroad Grade Trail, which you can then follow right 0.2 mile back to Fifteenmile Pass.

Another interesting way to reach Middle Tiger is via the Chirico Trail to West Side Road to the Hidden Forest Trail and then the 15 Mile Railroad Grade Trail. On the latter trail, expect some bushy sections as it winds through big trees, big boulders, and across a big bridge spanning a cascading creek. Then loop over the summit as described above. This trip is about 14.5 miles roundtrip, and solitude is guaranteed.

ISSAQUAH ALPS: TAYLOR & RATTLESNAKE MOUNTAINS

50 Taylor Mountain Forest

DISTANCE:	More than 20 miles of trails
ELEVATION GAIN:	Up to 2000 feet
HIGH POINT:	1625 feet
DIFFICULTY:	Easy to moderate
FITNESS:	Hikers, runners, cyclists
FAMILY-FRIENDLY:	Yes, but be aware of equestrian and mountain-bike use
DOG-FRIENDLY:	On leash
AMENITIES:	Privies
CONTACT/MAPS:	King County Parks; Green Trails Tiger Mountain/ Taylor Mountain No. 204S
BEFORE YOU GO:	Some trails are open seasonally; trails subject to change due to logging operations.
GPS:	N 47°25.983', W 121°58.251'

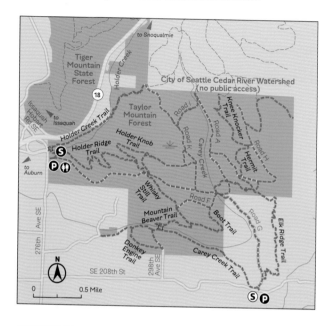

GETTING THERE

Driving: From Bellevue, follow I-405 south to I-90 and then head east, taking exit 17 in Issaquah. Turn right onto Front Street, which becomes the Issaquah Hobart Road SE (alternatively follow Newport Way NW to avoid downtown Issaquah congestion), and proceed for 8.7 miles to the State Route 18 interchange. Then continue straight, now on 276th Avenue SE, for 0.1 mile and turn left into the parking area and trailhead.

The forgotten Issaquah Alp, Taylor Mountain offers more than 20 miles of uncrowded trails and logging roads to roam free upon. While this county forest doesn't include Taylor's 2600-foot summit, it does include several ridges and knobs. It also contains large wetlands and two salmon spawning streams. Explore them and amble through forests of varied mixes and ages.

GET MOVING

Acquired by King County in 1997, the 1924-acre Taylor Mountain Forest provides an important habitat link between Tiger Mountain State Forest and the City of Seattle's Cedar River Municipal Watershed Ecological Reserve. The county manages this tract for environmentally sound forestry practices, ecosystem restoration, and passive recreation. A large and well-signed trail and road system (closed to public vehicles) traverses the property.

The Washington Trails Association and Back Country Horsemen of Washington, Tahoma Chapter, have assisted the county in building and maintaining these trails. Many of them are also open to mountain bikes. Despite this large trail system, use is pretty light, especially compared to nearby Tiger Mountain. Chances are good here for seeing elk, bears, and cougars.

From the trailhead most folks immediately head off for Holder Knob. Don't believe descriptions that extol this 1100-foot knoll's sweeping views of Mount Rainier. They aren't to be found. A feisty new forest has snuffed them out. Nevertheless, the lollipop loop hike to this knoll is enjoyable. The trail gently winds up a smaller knoll before dropping 100 feet to cross a creek in a ravine graced with big maples and cedars. Then it traverses Holder's south slopes to a junction. Here you can loop up and over the knob. There is a nice picnic spot and hitching post on the summit sans views. The total loop is 4.2 miles with about 800 feet of elevation gain.

You can greatly extend your hike by branching off this loop onto radiating logging roads or the Whisky Still Trail, which leads to the Boot and Mountain Beaver Trails. The latter descends to the Carey Creek valley, crossing the creek on a big bridge and coming to a junction. Here trails head west and south to other trailheads favored by local users. The attractive Carey Creek Trail heads east for 1.3 miles, following alongside the salmon-spawning waterway through mossy vine maples

Elk Ridge Trail

and cedar and spruce groves. It then follows a tributary to enter one of the few areas of Seattle's Cedar River Watershed that is open to the public (stay on the trail). Reach another trailhead (parking) off of SE 208th Street.

From this trailhead, you can head north on the recently reconstructed Elk Ridge Trail. This path winds through big trees and climbs a long ridge, reaching the Hermit Trail (with peekaboo views of Rainier) and Road H in about 1.4 miles. Here in the quiet and remote northeast corner of the forest, you can continue north on Road H or the Hermit and Knee Knocker Trails. It's possible to form a loop here—but to do so requires following poorly marked and poorly maintained trails on adjacent timberlands owned by Forterra. King County has plans to eventually develop a large loop trail around Taylor Mountain Forest, involving the Forterra land. In the meantime, only attempt exploring this area if you have excellent navigational skills.

One thing you will soon notice if you do some extensive exploring here is that many of the logging roads have recently had their culverts removed. While this aids salmon propagation, it can hinder foot travel. Some of the crossings can be quite wet and muddy outside of summer.

You can make a grand loop of the forest by following the Holder Ridge Trail to Whisky Still, Boot, Mountain Beaver, Carey Creek, and Elk Ridge Trails. Then follow Road H to Road A and walk north to Road I. Cross Carey Creek in an attractive grove and head west on this old road to Road K. Before heading north on Road K, consider strolling south a little way to check out the extensive wetlands along its west side. Then close your loop on the Holder Creek Trail, which involves a rocky, steep descent, boot-wetting fords of the creek and a tributary, and a lovely bridged crossing of Holder Creek. This grand circuit will yield you 9.5 miles and more than 2000 feet of elevation gain to record in your hiking or running log.

51 Rattlesnake Ledge and Mountain Traverse

DISTANCE:	Ledge: 4.2 miles roundtrip; Mountain Traverse: 10.7 miles one-way
ELEVATION GAIN:	Ledge: 1160 feet; Mountain Traverse: 2600 feet
HIGH POINT:	Ledge: 2079 feet; Mountain Traverse: 3517 feet
DIFFICULTY:	Moderate
FITNESS:	Runners, hikers
FAMILY-FRIENDLY:	Not suitable for young children because of sheer drops
DOG-FRIENDLY:	On leash
AMENITIES:	Privies, benches, picnic tables
CONTACT/MAPS:	King County Parks; Green Trails Rattlesnake Mountain/Snoqualmie Valley No. 205S
BEFORE YOU GO:	Rattlesnake Lake Trailhead parking lot often fills on weekends and is gated at dusk (check posted time). Do not park along road. Additional parking available at nearby Iron Horse State Park (Discover Pass required). Discover Pass required at Snoqualmie Point Trailhead. No pass required in nearby Snoqualmie Point Park. Parking lot closes near sunset (check posted time).
GPS:	N 47°26.103', W 121°46.144'

GETTING THERE

Driving: *Rattlesnake Lake Trailhead:* From Bellevue, follow I-90 east to exit 32. Then turn right onto 436th Avenue SE (which becomes Cedar Falls Road SE) and drive 3 miles, turning right for the trailhead parking. *Snoqualmie Point Park Trailhead:* From Bellevue, follow I-90 east to exit 27. Then turn right onto Winery Road and proceed for 0.3 mile. Next turn right and drive 0.1 mile to the trailhead and parking. Alternative parking is available at nearby Snoqualmie Point.

Climb to a precipitous ledge overlooking a deep blue lake and providing stunning views of three grand, glacier-scoured

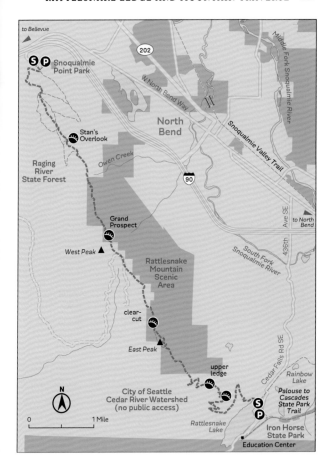

valleys on the Cascade Front. This is one of the busiest trails in the state so prepare to share the ledge with a multitude of folks. Go beyond the ledge and escape the crowds. Hike to more ledges, broad summits, ridgeline viewpoints, and forests of varying ages from recently cut to old-growth. And nowhere on any of these trails do you need to be concerned about rattlesnakes.

GET MOVING

RATTLESNAKE LEDGE

There are no rattlesnakes anywhere to be found here (or throughout western Washington). The mountain takes its name from early pioneers who thought they heard rattling snakes—but what they heard was probably rattling leaves. So hike this area free from venomous snake worry—but do exercise extreme caution on the ledge. The drop is precipitous: more than 400 feet. The ledge is extremely dangerous in wintery conditions—and a handful of hikers have perished here. Dogs should (and are required to) be on a leash. Keep children close.

To reach Rattlesnake Ledge, locate the trailhead near the parking lot entrance. It begins as a gated service road. Walk this level trail 0.3 mile around the northern tip of Rattlesnake Lake to a junction. Here a lineup of privies attests to this trail's popularity. Head right on a well-trodden and well-built (thanks to the Washington Trails Association) trail. Pass an old road heading right and an incredibly large glacial erratic. The trail then makes a long, sweeping switchback and gentle traverse beneath the ledge (look up for a glimpse of it).

Then the way gets down to business, steadily gaining elevation and utilizing shorter switchbacks. At just shy of 2.1 miles and more than 1100 feet of elevation gain, reach a junction. Head right, immediately emerging onto the exposed precipitous ledge. Catch your breath and watch your step. Stay well away from the ledge's edge and a deep fissure. Savor the sweeping view of Mount Si, Mailbox Peak, Mount Washington, and the three deep, U-shaped valleys they watch over. Notice the abrupt drop at the head of each valley—terminal moraine heaps left over from the Ice Age glaciers that scoured them.

Admire Rattlesnake Lake below, which hides a few remnants of the town of Moncton. In 1915 the lake's waters flooded due to seepage from the nearby, newly formed Chester Morse Lake on Cedar River. The town was destroyed

Hiker enjoying sweeping view of Rattlesnake Lake and Chester Morse Lake from the upper ledge

and abandoned. You can see a little of the Chester Morse Lake reservoir. The Cedar River provides the Seattle area with 70 percent of its water needs. Take a break to look down on the ledge, noticing penstemon and other flowers tenaciously growing in this harsh environment.

Above, there are two more ledges, with the upper one providing an even better view of the Cedar River valley. To reach them, return to the junction and continue steeply climbing—reaching the small middle ledge in about 0.2 mile, and the upper ledge in another 0.2 mile. Exercise extreme caution on these two exposed vantages.

RATTLESNAKE MOUNTAIN TRAVERSE

To do the full traverse, it's best to go from west to east, utilizing a gentler climb and saving the best views for the end. But if you want to savor peace and quiet, you might prefer to go from east to west, leaving the crowds behind early in the hike. A general description of the full traverse is given below from west to east.

Start at the Snoqualmie Point Park Trailhead, which is the same trailhead used by mountain bikers to access the Raging River State Forest mountain-bike trail network, so expect some initial company. But it's brief, as the Rattlesnake Mountain Trail is hiker-only. The bikers have their own trail network. You'll cross a couple of their tracks along the way. You'll immediately cross a logging road too—and a couple of others along the way. All road and trail intersections are well marked.

The trail starts out in a nearly all-deciduous forest, resembling a scene from back east. The trail is well graded and the tread smooth—two attributes I find desirable for running. Steadily ascending the broad mountain, reach a powerline swath at 1.9 miles—good views here west to the Olympics. At 2.4 miles you'll reach Stan's Overlook (elev. 2100 feet), the first of several viewpoints losing their views due to encroaching greenery. Nevertheless, you can make out Mounts Baker and Pilchuck in the distance.

The way soon leaves state forest and enters the 1771-acre Rattlesnake Mountain Scenic Area, a Natural Resources Conservation Area comanaged and co-owned by the Washington State Department of Natural Resources and King County. Now wind through attractive stands of mature conifers, including a couple of patches of old-growth forest. The way is easy going, traversing a gently sloping ridge. Slightly descend into a small gap to cross Owen Creek, and then steadily continue climbing. The way rolls over a knoll and follows a road for a short distance.

At 4.9 miles come to Grand Prospect (elev. 3000 feet), with its good but growing-in view north across the Snoqualmie Valley. Stand on the benches for a better vantage. The way then skirts the communication-towered West Peak and briefly leaves the scenic area. Now skirt and cross a new clear-cut providing excellent views south to Mount Rainier and west to East Tiger Mountain and the Olympics. Continue ascending, returning to the Scenic Area and older timber. You can skip the Windy Landing viewpoint until some wind topples some trees to open up the view.

At 6.7 miles reach a road on the East Peak. The trail continues across it—but first walk left a few feet to a bench and excellent view of Mounts Si and Teneriffe and the Middle Fork Snoqualmie Valley. The trail then skirts just below the 3517-foot forested high point of the mountain and begins its long descent to Rattlesnake Lake. Cross a logging road a couple of times and then begin to lose elevation more earnestly. At 8.3 miles reach the upper Rattlesnake Ledge, in my opinion the best viewpoint on the entire mountain. Then steeply descend, passing the other two ledges and legions of hikers, reaching the Rattlesnake Lake Trail at 10.7 miles.

GO FARTHER
Consider walking the short and pleasant Rattlesnake Lake Trail along the lakeshore to the Cedar River Watershed Education Center.

Next page: *Snoqualmie Valley Views at Tolt River-John MacDonald Park (Trail 55)*

SNOQUALMIE VALLEY

The Snoqualmie River threads together the communities of Duvall, Carnation, Fall City, Snoqualmie, and North Bend. Lying on the urban fringe and within the foothills of the Cascades, these east King County communities, especially Carnation and Fall City, have retained much of their rural charm. Snoqualmie (population 14,000) is the largest of these communities owing to its huge developments on a ridge south of its old town. But within that planned development are miles of trails.

Beyond these small towns' historic centers and new housing developments, you can still find large tracts of farmland and working forest. The valley is graced with several large parks and preserves containing miles of trails. And one of King County's longest rail trails runs the length of the valley, tying together the five communities.

52 Ring Hill Forest

DISTANCE:	2.7 miles of trails
ELEVATION GAIN:	Up to 200 feet
HIGH POINT:	525 feet
DIFFICULTY:	Easy
FITNESS:	Runners, hikers, cyclists
FAMILY-FRIENDLY:	Yes
DOG-FRIENDLY:	On leash
AMENITIES:	Benches
CONTACT/MAPS:	Ring Hill Forest (King County)
GPS:	N 47°44.721', W 122°01.762'

GETTING THERE

Driving: From Bellevue, follow I-405 north for 1 mile. Then take the exit for State Route 520 east. After 6.3 miles, SR 520 becomes Avondale Road NE. Continue straight on Avondale Road NE for 1 mile and bear right onto NE Novelty Hill Road. Stay on NE Novelty Hill Road for 3.5 miles and then turn left onto Trilogy Parkway NE. Continue for 1.2 miles and turn right onto 232nd Avenue NE. Then drive 2 miles north, coming to the trailhead and a small parking area on your right (just past the NE 162nd Street intersection).

Stroll along easy trails through a quiet forest on a broad hilltop above the Snoqualmie Valley. Acting as a buffer between suburban developments and rural agricultural lands, 320-acre Ring Hill Forest protects a forested plateau and steep, forested ravines above a fertile floodplain. A mixture of forest species and ages reflects Ring Hill's logging history.

GET MOVING

Not a park, but a working resource land, the Ring Hill Forest is off most people's recreational radar. But while this forest was established to protect a working forest and to provide a natural boundary between farmlands and housing lots, it's also open to passive recreation. Ring Hill contains just shy of 3 miles of trails open to hiking, mountain biking, and horse-back riding. The trail system is a tad short for most bicy-clists and equestrians—and most hikers are not aware of this property—so you can often expect to be alone here for your amblings.

From the small parking lot, follow a wide trail—formerly a logging road—reaching an unmarked but obvious junction in 0.25 mile. Here the main trail continues straight on a fairly level and grassy route, reconnecting with the trails leading

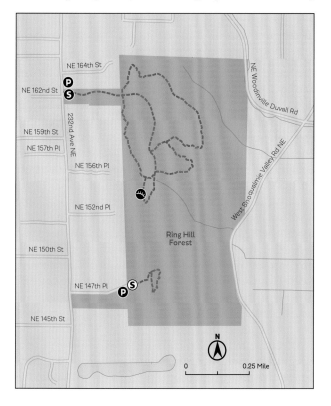

Lush canopy and understory at Ring Hill Forest

north and south from this junction. Head out on a loop or two of your making. You can easily hike all the trails here with just a little overlap for a good one- to two-hour outing.

The longest loop you can make from this spot is about 1.7 miles. Add the approach and exit, and you have a 2.2-mile hike. The terrain is fairly level, with only a few minor dips. The trails leading east of the main trail travel along the lip of the hilltop. They offer glimpses down steep slopes and ravines. There are several small bridges across seasonal creeks. And while the forest was logged in 1911 and again in the 1960s, there are some sizable maples, cedars, and hemlocks remaining. The county performs some small-scale sustainable forestry here, aiming for a healthy and diverse forest. Ring Hill is recovering quite nicely from past harvests. This is most noticeable at the "overlook." Enjoy the view shown on the interpretive sign, for the actual view has long been obscured by new forest growth.

If you desire to walk some more, there is a separate trailhead located at the end of NE 147th Place. Here you can head out on a very short lollipop loop of less than 0.5 mile. The trail is in excellent shape and nearly level. The forest is pretty mature and the way passes near a small creek cascading into a ravine. It also passes a large stump sporting what appears to be old railroad ties. Could they be the remains of an old logging railroad line? A section of trail here certainly looks like it could have once been a rail bed.

53 Lower Snoqualmie Valley Trail

DISTANCE:	18.8 miles one-way
ELEVATION GAIN:	350 feet
HIGH POINT:	500 feet
DIFFICULTY:	Easy
FITNESS:	Walkers, runners, hikers, cyclists
FAMILY-FRIENDLY:	Yes, and jogging stroller–friendly; be aware that trail is shared with horses and bikes
DOG-FRIENDLY:	On leash
AMENITIES:	Privies, benches, water, interpretive signs
CONTACT/MAPS:	King County Parks; Green Trails Rattlesnake Mountain/Snoqualmie Valley No. 205S (partial)
GPS:	N 47°44.669', W 121°59.177'

GETTING THERE

Driving: *Duvall Park and Ride Trailhead:* From Bellevue, follow I-405 north for 1 mile. Then take the exit for State Route 520 east. After 6.3 miles, SR 520 becomes Avondale Road NE. Continue straight on Avondale Road NE for 1 mile and bear right onto NE Novelty Hill Road. Stay on NE Novelty Hill Road for 4.7 miles and bear left onto West Snoqualmie Road NE. Continue north on this road (passing through a traffic light) for 2.9 miles. Then turn right onto NE Woodinville Duvall Road and drive 1.1 miles. Turn left on SR 203 (Main Street NE) and soon turn left into the Duvall Park and Ride for trailhead parking. (Additional parking is at nearby Depot Park.).

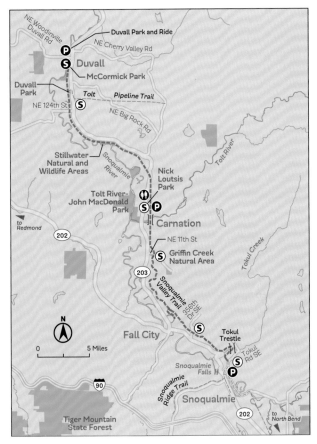

Nick Loutsis Park, Carnation: From Bellevue, follow I-405 north for 1 mile. Then take the exit for SR 520 and follow SR 520 east for 5.9 miles. Take the exit for SR 202 (Redmond Way) and head east (right) on SR 202. Continue for 7.7 miles and turn left onto NE Tolt Hill Road. Drive 3.2 miles and turn left onto SR 203 (Fall City-Carnation Road NE). After 0.8 mile, turn right onto Entwistle Street and proceed 0.3 mile to the trailhead at the park.

Transit: *Duvall Park and Ride Trailhead:* King County Metro lines 224, 232. *Nick Loutsis Park, Carnation:* King County Metro line 629 stops along SR 203 near the trail.

Hike, run, or walk one of the region's longest trails, passing through one of King County's loveliest remaining rural landscapes. Travel along riverbanks, cross wetlands and oxbow ponds, and meander around meadows, pastures, farms, and sprawling woodlots harboring stately trees. Pass through a couple of quaint communities and thrill in crossing a towering, historic trestle bridge spanning a ravine cradling a cascading creek.

GET MOVING

The Snoqualmie Valley Trail (SVT) consists of nearly 30 miles of a former line of the famed Chicago, Milwaukee, St. Paul and Pacific Railroad, also known as the Milwaukee Road. In the 1980s, nearly all of the line within the county was converted to trail. However, from Tokul Road SE to SE Reining Road near Snoqualmie, a nearly 2-mile stretch of the original line remains private property, requiring a 2.5-mile road detour.

Here the lower section of the trail is described. (See Trail 60 for a description of the upper section of the trail.) There are many access points (with parking) along the way. The two best points for short or moderate day hikes, walks, or runs along the trail are from the two parking areas mentioned above—both containing ample parking and trailhead facilities. The trail makes for an excellent one-way long hike or ultra-run too. If this sounds enticing to you, consider heading from east to west for a downhill start.

Following is a brief description of the trail from northwest to southeast. From the Duvall Park and Ride, the soft-surface trail passes beneath the NE Woodinville Duvall Road and skirts the community of Duvall. It passes through McCormick Park, where nature trails and a sandbar on the Snoqualmie

River may entice you to veer off course. The SVT also passes through the Duvall Dog Park and Duvall Park (alternative starts) and cuts across fertile Snoqualmie River floodplain. Half-mile/kilometer posts along the way may confuse you, as they are based on the distance from the Snohomish–King County boundary. Someday the trail may continue north to the boundary and beyond.

At 2.5 miles carefully cross busy NE 124th Street. The SVT then runs pretty close to SR 203 and the Snoqualmie River. Eventually, the trail pulls away from the road and traverses King County's Stillwater Natural Area and Washington Department of Fish and Wildlife's Stillwater Unit. Here cross a lush, pretty floodplain of farmlands, wetlands, and oxbow ponds. Wildlife is rich. Watch for an assortment of birds and small mammals. And be aware that hunting is allowed in season here.

Tokul Trestle

The trail travels over several small trestles and passes a couple of trailheads (Discover Pass required) before crossing a large field and coming to busy SR 203 at 7.4 miles. Carefully cross the highway and continue on a near straightaway to Nick Loutsis Park (parking, water, privy) in Carnation, just after crossing Entwistle Street at 8.8 miles.

Now continue on a well-walked section of trail, coming to a big bridge spanning the Tolt River at 9.2 miles. Here a trail heads right along the river to the Tolt River–John MacDonald Park (see Trail 55). The SVT continues south, skirting Camp Don Bosco and crossing a creek and road via restored trestles. It then traverses attractive forest, coming to King County's Griffin Creek Natural Area and a trailhead on dirt NE 11th Street at 10.9 miles.

The trail crosses Griffin Creek and begins a long, gradual ascent off the floodplain, traversing heavily wooded slopes. Come to two more trestles over cascading creeks. At 14 miles reach a signed junction. Here a closed-to-vehicles road descends to Fall City. This road is used by mountain bikers to access the extensive series of trails within the Tokul West network. Hikers may want to check out some of the multiuse trails (be aware of heavy mountain-bike use), but a permit is required as these trails are on private forest land (contact Campbell Global properties).

The SVT continues its gradual ascent. At 15.7 miles, reach 356th Drive SE and a busy trailhead favored by mountain bikers accessing the Tokul East trail network. The SVT crosses working forests while it continues to gain elevation. At 18 miles reach the trail's highlight, the Tokul Trestle. Built in 1911, this recently rehabilitated, 400-foot-long wooden trestle curves and towers 120 feet over Tokul Creek. Take your time sauntering across it, savoring the sounds of the crashing creek below and taking in sweet views of the Issaquah Alps across the valley.

Beyond the trestle, the lower SVT skirts more working forests, coming to its eastern terminus (parking) at 18.8 miles at the Tokul Tunnel (an underpass) on Tokul Road SE. Beyond, the original right-of-way crosses private property and is closed to the public.

54 Moss Lake Natural Area

DISTANCE:	About 3 miles of trails
ELEVATION GAIN:	Up to 100 feet
HIGH POINT:	630 feet
DIFFICULTY:	Easy
FITNESS:	Walkers, runners, hikers
FAMILY-FRIENDLY:	Yes, and some trails suitable for jogging strollers
DOG-FRIENDLY:	On leash
AMENITIES:	Privies
CONTACT/MAPS:	King County Parks
GPS:	N 47°41.531', W 121°51.206'

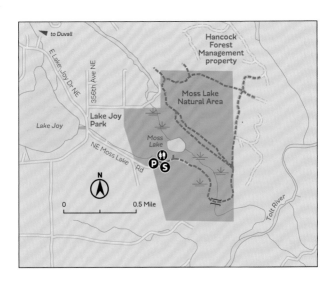

Taking a break for a little play at Moss Lake

GETTING THERE

Driving: From Bellevue, follow I-405 north for 1 mile. Then take the exit for State Route 520 east. After 6.3 miles, SR 520 becomes Avondale Road NE. Continue straight on Avondale Road NE for 1 mile and bear right onto NE Novelty Hill Road. Stay on NE Novelty Hill Road for 4.7 miles and bear left onto West Snoqualmie Road NE. Continue north for 0.3 mile and turn right onto NE 124th Street. Then drive 1 mile to a roundabout. Exit right on SR 203 (Fall City Duvall Road) and drive 3.8 miles. Turn left onto NE Stillwater Hill Road (which becomes Kelley Road NE) and continue 2 miles. Bear right onto NE Lake Joy Road and after 1.8 miles bear left onto E. Lake Joy Drive NE. Drive 0.7 mile and turn left onto NE Moss Lake Road. Continue 0.5 mile to the trailhead.

Take to quiet trails skirting a sprawling sphagnum bog and traversing quiet upland forest. More than 40 percent of the 372-acre Moss Lake Natural Area consists of wetlands, making it a prime spot for observing amphibians, birds, and other wild critters. Look for eagles, beavers, and herons. Mosquitos can sometimes be a concern, but crowds never are. You have an excellent chance of being alone in this ecologically significant preserve.

GET MOVING

The first major purchase under King County's 1989 open space bond, Moss Lake's extensive peat bog is a county rarity. The area was long used for peat mining—from the 1920s until the 1960s. The little lake, which is surrounded by bog, was probably formed from the mining. Until recently, most of the property remained recreationally unenhanced. But King County Parks, with the help of the Washington Trails Association, has constructed a new trail on the property to complement its old roads.

From the parking area, walk past a gated, old road—now serving as the park's main trail. Within a little more than 0.1 mile, you'll come to a spur offering the only (and often muddy) access to the lake. This is a great spot to look for birds and launch a canoe. The road-trail continues, passing through lovely maple forest and along the bog edge, which is lined with salmonberries. Come in late spring and enjoy plump berries. Come in fall and enjoy a golden forest canopy.

Continue hiking to a new bridge spanning the lake's outlet stream, which feeds into the nearby Tolt River. At 0.9 mile come to a junction. Here two road-trails diverge and a 1.8-mile loop can be made. However, the trail to the right leaves county land to traverse private Hancock Forest Management property for 0.4 mile. The road left largely remains within the natural area, climbing above the bog and traversing upland forest for 1.3 miles. Beyond where the road-trail bends east, a couple of unmarked trails diverge left, heading for private timberland. These trails are primarily used by mountain bikers and equestrians.

A new trail splits from the road-trail not too far from the junction and travels closer to the bog. There are some good viewpoints of the sprawling wetland complex along the way and some benches for taking a break. It's a little more than a mile to make a loop utilizing this trail and the road-trail.

55 Tolt River-John MacDonald Park

DISTANCE:	More than 12 miles of trails
ELEVATION GAIN:	Up to 520 feet
HIGH POINT:	575 feet
DIFFICULTY:	Easy to moderate
FITNESS:	Walkers, runners, hikers, cyclists
FAMILY-FRIENDLY:	Yes, but be aware of mountain-bike use on some trails; some jogging stroller–friendly trails
DOG-FRIENDLY:	On leash
AMENITIES:	Privies, water, interpretive signs, picnic tables and shelters, campground, playfields
CONTACT/MAPS:	King County Parks
GPS:	N 47°38.628', W 121°55.486'

GETTING THERE

Driving: From Bellevue, follow I-405 north for 1 mile. Then take the exit for State Route 520 and follow SR 520 east for 5.9 miles. Take the exit for SR 202 (Redmond Way) and head east (right) on SR 202. Continue for 7.7 miles and turn left onto NE Tolt Hill Road. Drive 3.3 miles and turn left onto SR 203 (Fall City-Carnation Road NE). After 0.5 mile, turn left onto NE 40th Street and proceed 0.3 mile to the trailhead at the park.

   Transit: King County Metro line 629

Abutting the bucolic little town of Carnation is the lovely, large Tolt River-John MacDonald Park. Occupying 574 acres at the confluence of the Tolt and Snoqualmie Rivers, this park

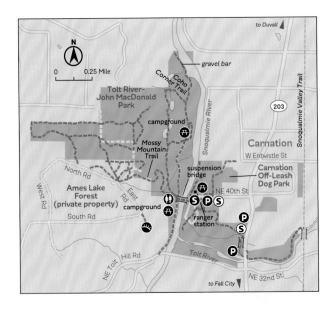

contains varied terrain and an array of trails. Explore mature forest groves, wildlife-rich wetlands, a rugged hill, and the dynamic banks of two large rivers. A large suspension bridge over the Snoqualmie River is a park highlight.

GET MOVING

Long a popular park with its campground and picnic grounds, Tolt-MacDonald is also a great hiking, mountain biking, and trail running destination. The upper trails can get busy at times with mountain-bike use, but there is a lot of room to roam. The park borders the private (but open to the public with an easement) Ames Lake Forest, adding another 10 miles or so of trail and forest roads to explore.

On the east side of the Snoqualmie River, find several miles of easy, primarily level trails. North of the parking area are old farm buildings (one now serving as a ranger station) and two trails. One trail runs along the Snoqualmie River for

0.3 mile, while another trail heads 0.35 mile by sports fields and the Carnation Off-Leash Dog Park to W. Entwistle Street in "downtown" Carnation. And be sure to check out the huge butternut tree (native to the eastern United States).

South of the parking area is a lovely paved trail perfect for jogging strollers and wheelchairs. It skirts a wetlands complex, crossing a few sloughs along the way before reaching a ballfield and parking area in 0.4 mile. The trail then continues 0.2 mile south to another parking area. From here you can continue on a wide gravel trail east, ducking under SR 203 and traveling along the Tolt River for 0.5 mile to the Snoqualmie Valley Trail (see Trail 53). It's lined with cottonwoods and bigleaf maples and is absolutely gorgeous in the autumn.

West of the parking and main camping area, take a 500-foot-long suspension bridge over the Snoqualmie River for more—a lot more—trails. From a meadow sporting yurts, shelters, and campsites, you can hike south on a service road along the river for 0.4 mile; or head north on a wide trail along the river, traversing meadows and groves of tall cottonwood and reaching a large gravel bar at 0.9 mile. You can return on the Coho Corner Trail, which crosses a wetland channel and climbs a steep bench above the floodplain. It returns to the meadow camping area in 1 mile.

To reach the upper trail network, walk to the west end of the campground to the Mossy Mountain Trail. Then follow this old skid road for 0.6 mile, skirting a ravine and climbing more than 400 feet to a major road-trail junction on a broad hilltop in the Ames Lake Forest. There are miles of unmarked, closed-to-vehicles roads and trails here, primarily used by mountain bikers. The forest is pretty scrappy or recently cut. But you may want to go left on East Road 0.3 mile to a short spur leading to the lookout. Here enjoy a beautiful view east overlooking the confluence of the Tolt and Snoqualmie Rivers, as well as out to the Cascade Front and Issaquah Alps.

If you're inclined, you can continue on the Ames Lake Forest's South, West, and North Roads for a loop of about 1.8 miles. To reach the park's well-maintained and well-signed upper trails, head out from the major junction north on a logging road. It steeply (but shortly) climbs, returning to the park and connecting with several trails. Then, with a map in hand, head out! If you follow trails along the periphery of the upper park, count on racking up at least 2 miles. Most of the way is level, but there are some dips and climbs, particularly along the northern boundary. There are plenty of connector trails to add loops and figure eights. You're guaranteed to get in a good workout.

While these trails are fairly popular, I was once stalked here by a cougar. Bears are frequently sighted here too. This area is still a little wild, despite its proximity to burgeoning Redmond.

Trail along the Tolt River

56 Preston-Snoqualmie Trail

DISTANCE:	11 miles roundtrip
ELEVATION GAIN:	500 feet
HIGH POINT:	520 feet
DIFFICULTY:	Easy
FITNESS:	Walkers, runners, hikers, cyclists
FAMILY-FRIENDLY:	Yes
DOG-FRIENDLY:	On leash
AMENITIES:	Privies, benches
CONTACT/MAPS:	King County Parks; Green Trails Rattlesnake Mountain/Snoqualmie Valley No. 205S
GPS:	N 47°31.337', W 121°56.079'

GETTING THERE

Driving: From Bellevue, follow I-90 east to exit 22. Then turn left on SE 82nd Street, cross the freeway, and turn right onto SE High Point Way. Drive 0.4 mile, turn left onto SE 87th Place, where you'll see the trailhead and parking on your right.

Transit: King County Metro line 628 stops at nearby Preston Park and Ride.

One of the Eastside's oldest paved rail trails, the Preston-Snoqualmie Trail is also one of its quieter ones. Walk or run through groves of towering firs, maples, and cottonwoods and traverse a forested ridge high above the Snoqualmie Valley. Cross the Raging River on an old highway bridge and try to sneak a peek of Snoqualmie Falls from a viewpoint rapidly being overcome by new greenery.

GET MOVING

Start from what once was the western terminus of the Preston-Snoqualmie Trail. Several years ago, the trail was

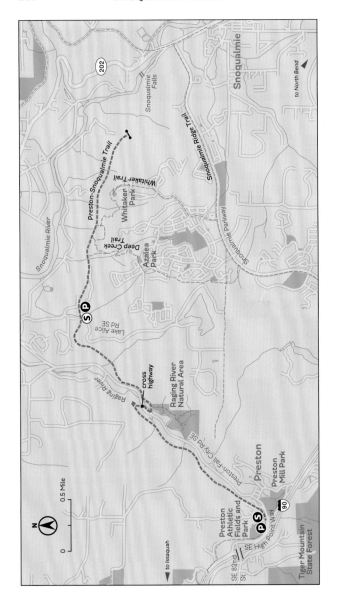

202

Snoqualmie Falls

Snoqualmie

to North Bend

Preston-Snoqualmie Trail

Snoqualmie Ridge Trail

Whitaker Trail

Whitaker Park

Snoqualmie River

Deep Creek Trail

Azalea Park

Shoqualmie Parkway

S P

Lake Alice Rd SE

cross highway

Raging River Natural Area

Raging River

Preston-Fall City Rd SE

0.5 Mile

Preston

Preston Mill Park

N

0   0.5 Mile

to Issaquah

Preston Athletic Fields and Park

P S

90

SE Highpoint Way

SE 82nd St

Tiger Mountain State Forest

extended west by 0.9 mile. It traverses the nearby Preston Athletic Fields and Park (alternative parking, restrooms, picnic tables) and then swings around some buildings, ending on SE High Point Way. Its main appeal is for cyclists using it in conjunction with the nearby Issaquah-Preston Trail (which parallels I-90). Feel free to walk or run it, but most folks immediately head east.

The trail, a former rail line for the Seattle, Lake Shore and Eastern Railway (from which Seattle's popular Burke-Gilman Trail was also born), begins a slow descent, skirting below a handful of old and well-kept homes from Preston's early mill town days. Pass a path and stairway on the right leading to the Preston Community Center, built in 1939 by the Works Progress Administration (WPA). The trail then leaves the small town, traversing steep, lush, forested slopes above the busy Preston-Fall City Road. Tall cedars, cottonwoods, maples, and Sitka spruce line the way.

Cross several small, cascading creeks, one on an original trestle. Unfortunately, the old trestle once spanning the Preston-Fall City Road and the Raging River is long gone. So here at 2 miles, the trail leaves the rail bed and steeply drops to cross the busy road. Use extreme caution, as drivers frequently speed through this crossing. The trail, now separated from the road by a concrete barrier, follows alongside it for a short distance. Cross the Raging River, a pretty sight for a rest break—then follow the Preston-Fall City Road again for a short distance.

The trail, now gravel, climbs via eight short switchbacks back to the rail bed. Then, paved once again, the going is easy and peaceful. The way crosses a creek via a high, old trestle and curves around a hillside. At 3.7 miles, come to Lake Alice Road SE and a trailhead (alternative start), complete with privy and parking for a dozen vehicles.

The trail then crosses the road and traverses wooded slopes above the Snoqualmie River. Pass a series of benches

Placid forest above the Raging River

where views of the valley below used to be wide, but trees and shrubbery are doing their darnedest to rein them in. At 4.2 miles, Deep Creek Trail ventures south into the forest. At 4.4 miles, reach Whitaker Trail. Both of these trails lead to neighborhoods within the Snoqualmie Ridge development (see Go Farther).

The Preston-Snoqualmie Trail continues for another 1.1 miles, coming to its end at a gate. Here find a privy, a picnic table, and three benches staring into the trees. The three benches used to look out at Snoqualmie Falls. No more—vegetation has reclaimed the view. You can wiggle around a little, trying to catch a glimpse. In winter, thinner foliage grants a little more viewing. In any case, you'll hear the nearby falls roaring.

It would be nice if the trestle beyond could someday be restored and this trail pushed all the way to Snoqualmie. For now, however, this is it.

GO FARTHER

The two trails leading from the Preston-Snoqualmie Trail are worth checking out. They are both wide and well built (although they can get muddy during the rainy months), and both climb more than 400 feet on their way to Snoqualmie Ridge. The Whitaker Trail crosses a cascading creek and then steeply climbs a ridge of young maples to Whitaker Park (with a growing-in view) before reaching SE Kendall Peak Street at 0.9 mile at a powerline swath. There is a good view here over the paved trail below and of the Snoqualmie River.

The Deep Creek Trail makes a bridged creek crossing and then steeply climbs through mature timber, passing some good-sized trees before reaching Azalea Park (parking, restroom, picnic table) at Douglas Avenue SE at 0.9 mile. There is also a 0.2-mile trail (signed Main Trail) connecting these two trails, allowing for a short loop from the Preston-Snoqualmie Trail. There are many other trails to explore throughout Snoqualmie Ridge as well.

57 Snoqualmie Falls

DISTANCE:	1.4 miles roundtrip
ELEVATION GAIN:	280 feet
HIGH POINT:	440 feet
DIFFICULTY:	Moderate
FITNESS:	Walkers
FAMILY-FRIENDLY:	Yes
DOG-FRIENDLY:	On leash
AMENITIES:	Restrooms, water, interpretive displays, benches
CONTACT/MAPS:	Puget Sound Energy; Green Trails Rattlesnake Mountain/Upper Snoqualmie Valley
BEFORE YOU GO:	Parking lot on west side of State Route 202 (close to gift shop) requires a fee. Parking area on east side of road is free.
GPS:	N 47°32.552', W 121°50.173'

GETTING THERE

Driving: From Bellevue, follow I-90 east to exit 25. Then head north on Snoqualmie Parkway for 3.7 miles. Turn left onto

State Route 202 (Railroad Avenue) and continue 0.6 mile. Immediately after passing beneath a covered walkway bridge, turn right into the trailhead parking.

Transit: King County Metro line 629

One of the state's top tourist attractions, Snoqualmie Falls is Washington's most famous waterfall and an iconic natural feature. It's a place residents visit frequently—often with friends and family from near and far. A short and steep but sweet trail leads from observatories above the falls to the base of the thundering waterfall in a narrow, rocky canyon. Take it, leaving the crowds, and fully experience the 268-foot waterfall from top to crashing bottom.

GET MOVING

More than 1.5 million admirers come to Snoqualmie Falls each year. Yet the far majority of them don't take the trail to the falls' bottom. One hundred feet taller than the famed Niagara Falls of New York and Ontario, like those national treasures,

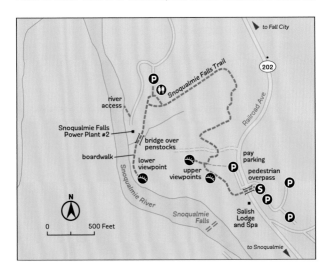

Snoqualmie Falls roar after winter and spring storms.

this one too was tapped for electricity production. A resort sits on the rim above it too—so don't come here looking for a pristine natural environment. In any case, the scene is gorgeous and nature does a pretty good job of shining through.

While the hike out and back is a mere 1.4 miles, do plan on spending some time here. Snoqualmie Falls is saturated with history, and this beautiful Puget Sound Energy park contains a lot of interpretive displays. To the Snoqualmie Tribe, these falls are the place where the first man and woman were created by Moon the Transformer. In the 1890s, civil engineer Charles Baker constructed an underground power plant (the first completely underground power plant in the world) at the falls (and those transformers are still in use). In 1911, a second power house was constructed.

From the parking lot, walk through a covered bridge over SR 202 and come to the upper observatories. While a good amount of the river is diverted for power production, the falls are always showy and impressive. After periods of heavy rainfall, they are downright spellbinding—and you will get wet watching them from above. While the falls will hold your attention, do scan the ridge directly across the river canyon for old trestle remnants (see Trail 56).

Before the last observatory, a soft-surface trail diverts right. It steeply descends through a mossy, often-misty mature forest. There are interpretive signs along the way. The path emerges at the lower parking lot (accessed from SR 202 via 372nd Avenue SW and SE Fish Hatchery Road) and restrooms. Here you can take a paved path to the river's edge or a boardwalk over the penstocks feeding the second power plant. The boardwalk then heads up a tight canyon to the base of the thundering falls. According to the Snoqualmie Tribe, the mists here at the base of the waterfall connect heaven and earth.

GO FARTHER

In nearby Snoqualmie, walk the paved 0.9-mile Centennial Trail through that town's historic depot and train yard. Children and train enthusiasts will love it.

58 Meadowbrook Farm

DISTANCE:	About 3 miles of trails
ELEVATION GAIN:	Minimal
HIGH POINT:	425 feet
DIFFICULTY:	Easy
FITNESS:	Walkers, runners
FAMILY-FRIENDLY:	Yes, and some trails jogging stroller–friendly
DOG-FRIENDLY:	On leash
AMENITIES:	Restrooms, water at adjacent Centennial Fields
CONTACT/MAPS:	Meadowbrook Farm Preservation Association; Green Trails Rattlesnake Mountain/Upper Snoqualmie Valley
BEFORE YOU GO:	Some trails are prone to flooding from late fall to early spring.
GPS:	N 47°30.528', W 121°47.985'

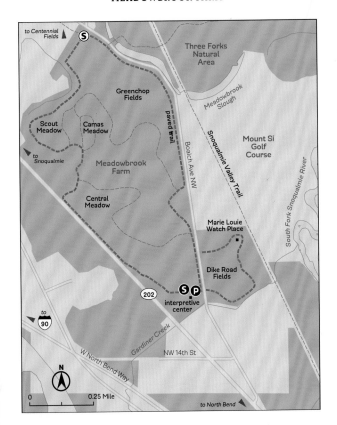

GETTING THERE

Driving: From Bellevue, follow I-90 east to exit 27. Turn left onto Winery Road (which becomes SE North Bend Way) and drive 1.1 miles. Then turn left onto Meadowbrook Way SE and continue for 0.7 mile. Turn right onto State Route 202 (Railroad Avenue, which becomes Snoqualmie North Bend Road) and continue for 0.7 mile. Turn left onto NW 14th Street, proceed 0.1 mile, and turn left onto Boalch Avenue NW. Continue for 0.3 mile and turn left into the parking area for Meadowbrook Farm Interpretive Center and the trailhead.

Transit: King County Metro line 208 stops at the corner of NW 14th Street and Boalch Avenue NW, 0.3 mile from the trailhead.

Amble through a historic and culturally significant prairie near the confluence of the three forks of the Snoqualmie River. Along a virtually flat landscape, savor stunning views of sur-rounding summits, including Mount Si majestically watching over the valley. Inspect wetland pools and creeks for aquatic life, and scan meadows for foraging elk. Admire a little art in the park and reflect on the lives of those who've shaped and have been shaped by this sublime landscape.

GET MOVING

According to oral tradition, this verdant prairie a short distance upriver from Snoqualmie Falls is the birthplace of

Grazing elk at Meadowbrook Farm

the Snoqualmie Tribe. Jeremiah Borst, a pioneer from Virginia, homesteaded the prairie with his Snoqualmie wife in 1858. In the 1880s, Borst sold his farm to the Hop Growers Association. It soon became one of the largest hops operations in the world. In 1904, the property became a large dairy farm. In the 1960s, the property was bought by a real-estate investment group, which began to subdivide it and develop parcels. In 1996, the core 460 acres of the historic farm were permanently preserved as open space.

There are about 3 miles of trails within the farm, but only half of them are well developed. From the interpretive center (open for classes, events. and group rentals), two trails—one paved and one graveled—set off along the farm's periphery. The graveled path follows the farm's southwest boundary along the Central Meadow. Views across the meadow of iconic Mount Si are divine. Look for elk, which have been rebounding in this valley. And always keep a safe distance from these large members of the deer family.

The trail passes an attractive mountain identifier and then becomes a primitive path on its way to Camas Meadow. Look for these showy flowers in late spring. The path continues via an old farm path to Scout Meadow, where it turns north to connect with the paved path. The paved path runs for 1.1 miles, from the interpretive center to the adjacent Centennial Fields (restrooms, water, and parking). There is a short paved loop here. You can also access (across SE Park Street) a 0.2-mile path through a dog park. The path connects with the Snoqualmie Valley Trail (see Trail 60) and continues for another 0.6 mile through the Three Forks Natural Area.

The paved path parallels the road for a good portion of its course. Around midway, it crosses a couple of creeks and travels via boardwalk across a wet meadow. Enjoy good views of Rattlesnake Mountain. A complete loop around the farm is about 2.3 miles. East of Boalch Avenue NW near the interpretive center, find a short loop trail around Dike Road Fields. The

highlight on this trail is the Marie Louie Watch Place art installation. Honoring Louie, an early Snoqualmie medicine woman,
this set of eleven articulated cedar posts marks the sunrise
direction through the calendar cycle.

GO FARTHER

Combine with the nearby Tollgate Farm Park (see Trail 59).

59 Tollgate Farm Park

DISTANCE:	1.5 miles of trails
ELEVATION GAIN:	Minimal
HIGH POINT:	435 feet
DIFFICULTY:	Easy
FITNESS:	Walkers, runners
FAMILY-FRIENDLY:	Yes, and jogging stroller–friendly
DOG-FRIENDLY:	On leash
AMENITIES:	Restrooms, picnic tables, benches, interpretive signs
CONTACT/MAPS:	Si View Metropolitan District
GPS:	N 47°30.120', W 121°47.970'

GETTING THERE

Driving: From Bellevue, follow I-90 east to exit 27. Turn left
onto Winery Road (which becomes SE North Bend Way) and
drive 2.5 miles. Then turn left into Tollgate Farm Park for
parking and the trailhead.

Transit: King County Metro line 208 stops on Bendigo
Boulevard, where the trail can be accessed.

Walk through a historic prairie that sustained Native peoples, was among the first homesteads in the Snoqualmie Valley, and was the site of a toll booth on the Snoqualmie Pass
Wagon Road. Saved from development in 2001 and opened
as a park in 2015, Tollgate Farm Park is easily one of the most
beautiful and idyllic locations within the Snoqualmie Valley.

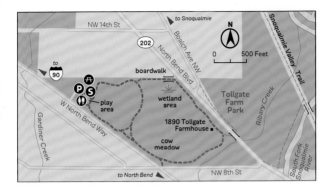

GET MOVING

Known among many local residents as the Cow Park for its resident bovine herd, Tollgate Farm Park retains a semblance of its agricultural past. Only a small portion of the 400-plus-acre park is developed, with a small parking lot, playground, and picnic area. The rest of the property is open space, with two loop trails, a spur trail, and a restored farmhouse from the 1890s.

Much of the park is a historic prairie near the South Fork of the Snoqualmie River. The views of Mount Si rising above it are breathtaking, and your eyes will be fixated on this iconic valley peak during much of your visit. Views are good too of Rattlesnake Mountain to the south and Mount Washington, Mailbox Peak, and other Snoqualmie Pass peaks to the east.

Take to the park's loop trail, traveling along the periphery of the prairie. The path parallels W. North Bend Way, weaving through a row of apple trees and other hardwoods. If you're just looking for a short walk, take to the 0.5-mile loop. If you want more, follow the longer loop for a 1-mile trip around the core of the historic farm. Nearly level, this gravel path with a short boardwalk section is a pure delight to walk for park users of all ages. And while it's only a mile, you'll want to take your time, especially if this is your first visit.

Mount Si provides a stunning backdrop to Tollgate Farm Park.

Stop at the numerous attractive interpretive signs and learn about this property's fascinating past. Occupying a prairie important to Native peoples, this site was homesteaded in 1867. In 1865, the historic Snoqualmie Pass Wagon Road was cut through this property. In 1883, it became a toll road, and a toll house was set up here—hence the farm's name. The 1890-built Tollgate Farmhouse still graces the property. You'll walk right past this recently renovated building.

GO FARTHER

Near the farmhouse, a 0.2-mile spur trail leads north along Ribary Creek, ducking under State Route 202. It then swings west, ending on Boalch Avenue NW. From here you can walk that quiet road 0.6 mile to Meadowbrook Farm (see Trail 58). You can also walk across the SR 202 Ribary Creek Bridge (pedestrian lane) and then carefully walk the road shoulder a short distance to a trail leading north along the South Fork Snoqualmie River to reach the Snoqualmie Valley Trail (see Trail 60) in 0.4 mile.

60 Upper Snoqualmie Valley Trail

DISTANCE:	9.4 miles one-way
ELEVATION GAIN:	550 feet
HIGH POINT:	960 feet
DIFFICULTY:	Easy
FITNESS:	Walkers, runners, hikers, cyclists
FAMILY-FRIENDLY:	Yes, and jogging stroller–friendly
DOG-FRIENDLY:	On leash
AMENITIES:	Privies, benches, water, interpretive signs
CONTACT/MAPS:	King County Parks; Green Trails Rattlesnake Mountain/Snoqualmie Valley No. 205S
BEFORE YOU GO:	Eastern trailhead is near Rattlesnake Lake at the Palouse to Cascades State Park Trail, requiring a Discover Pass. Additional parking available at nearby Rattlesnake Lake Trailhead (no pass required, but parking lot often fills on weekends; do not park along road). Parking lots gated at dusk (check posted time).
GPS:	N 47°29.598', W 121°46.633'

GETTING THERE

Driving: *Torguson Park:* From Bellevue, follow I-90 east to exit 31. Go through a roundabout, exiting onto Bendigo Boulevard S. (State Route 202). After 0.6 mile, turn right onto W. Park Street and drive 0.3 mile. Then turn right onto SE North Bend Way and continue for 0.3 mile. Turn left into the park for the trailhead and parking. *Eastern Trailhead:* From Bellevue, follow I-90 east to exit 32. Then turn right onto 436th Avenue SE (which becomes Cedar Falls Road SE) and drive 3.1 miles, turning left for trailhead parking at the Palouse to Cascades State Park Trail near Rattlesnake Lake.

Transit: *Torguson Park:* King County Metro line 628 stops on North Bend Boulevard N. and Bendigo Boulevard N., close to the trail.

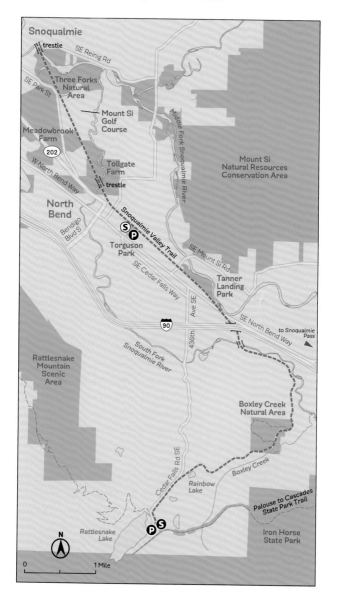

Hike, run, or walk along a former railroad line passing through historic farms, wildlife-rich wetlands and oxbow ponds, and the heart of North Bend. Enjoy inspiring views of valley landmark Mount Si keeping watch over the Snoqualmie Valley. And enjoy a couple of river crossings on old trestle bridges.

GET MOVING

The upper Snoqualmie Valley Trail (SVT) offers an entirely different experience than the lower trail. Part of the same rail line, the trail is truncated by almost 2 miles (requiring a 2.5-mile road walk to connect) near Snoqualmie, where a large mill once operated. The upper trail offers more mountain views and includes a long uphill stretch on its way to its eastern terminus at Rattlesnake Lake.

The western reaches make for the best short runs and walks on this trail. Parking is available but limited near the western terminus. Torguson Park, with its ample parking, good facilities, and proximity to North Bend, is a logical place to start. If a one-way trip is on your mind, it's best to start at Rattlesnake Lake and head west, taking advantage of a long downhill start.

From west to east, the trail starts on SE Reinig Road with a stair climb to a trestle bridge spanning the Snoqualmie River. It then traverses the Three Forks Natural Area, coming to a junction at 0.5 mile. Right leads through a dog park, reaching a trailhead on SE Park Street near Centennial Fields (see Trail 58). Left leads about 0.6 mile through the natural area.

The trail continues straight, crossing Meadowbrook Slough and coming to the Mount Si Golf Course at 0.8 mile. Enjoy close-up views of Mount Si hovering above. Pass through a large gate meant to keep resident elk out and traverse the course, watching for eagles and other birdies. Exit the course through another elk gate and traverse wetlands at the edge of Tollgate Farm. At 2.1 miles, reach a trail just before a bridge spanning the South Fork Snoqualmie River. It heads

Young cyclist admiring the Snoqualmie River

0.5 mile to North Bend Boulevard and Tollgate Farm (see Trail 59).

The SVT then crosses the river and reaches North Bend, crossing a series of mostly lightly traveled roads. At 2.8 miles reach Torguson Park. The SVT continues southeast on a level straightaway. At 3.8 miles cross SE Mount Si Road (use caution). The trail then brushes up alongside the Middle Fork Snoqualmie River before bending south and crossing the very busy (use more caution) SE North Bend Way at 4.7 miles.

The SVT then ducks beneath I-90, crosses the South Fork Snoqualmie River, and parallels it for a short stint before starting its uphill grind. At 6.4 miles, cross a powerline swath providing a good view of Mailbox Peak and Mount Washington. The trail then traverses quiet woodlands above Boxley Creek and passes through the Boxley Creek Natural Area—where a short loop trail can be explored. The SVT then skirts Rainbow Lake and some large wetlands before terminating at the Rattlesnake Recreation Area at 9.4 miles.

GO FARTHER

From Rattlesnake Lake you have a choice of many more trails, including Rattlesnake Ledge (see Trail 51) and the Palouse to Cascades State Park Trail—formerly known as the John Wayne Pioneer Trail—which travels nearly 300 miles across the state (and out of the scope of this book)!

ACKNOWLEDGMENTS

RESEARCHING AND WRITING *Urban Trails: Eastside* was fun, gratifying, and a lot of hard work. I couldn't have finished this project without the help and support of the following people. A huge thank you to all the great people at Mountaineers Books, especially publisher, Helen Cherullo; editor-in-chief, Kate Rogers; and project manager, Melissa Kiepke.

A big thank you to my editor Emily Barnes for her attention to detail and thoughtful suggestions, helping to make this book a finer volume. I also want to thank my wife, Heather, and son, Giovanni, for accompanying me on many of the trails in this book. A big thanks too to Tami Asars, Jennifer and James Bradwin, Suzanne Gerber, Lee Jacobson, Maryna Kedo, Judith Romano, Virginia Scott, Emily White, and Bob Wismer for providing me with excellent trail company. And I thank God for watching over me and keeping me safe and healthy while I hiked, biked, and ran all over the Eastside!

RESOURCES

CONTACTS AND MAPS

City of Bellevue
Bellevue Botanical Garden
(425) 452-2750
www.bellevuebotanical.org

City of Bellevue Parks and
Community Services
https://parks.bellevuewa.gov
/parks-and-trails and see the
sections listed below. Exceptions
noted below.

Coal Creek Natural Area
(425) 452-6885
See Nature Trails on website.

Kelsey Creek Farm Park
https://parks.bellevuewa.gov
/community-centers
/kelsey-creek-farm

Lake Hills Greenbelt
(425) 452-6885
See Nature Trails on website.

Lake to Lake Trail
See Nature Trails on website.

Lakemont Park
(425) 452-6885
See Nature Trails on website.

Lewis Creek Park
(425) 452-4195
See Parks on website.

Mercer Slough Nature Park
(425) 452-2565
See Parks on website.

Robinswood Park
(425) 452-6885
See Parks on website.

Wilburton Hill Park
(425) 452-6885
See Parks on website.

Weowna Park
See Parks on website.

City of Kirkland
Cross Kirkland Corridor
(425) 587-3875
www.kirklandwa.gov/Residents
/Community/Cross_Kirkland
_Corridor.htm

City of Kirkland Parks and
Community Services
www.kirklandwa.gov/depart
/parks.htm and see the Online
Parks Guide in Parks and Open
Spaces for the parks listed below.

Juanita Bay Park

Juanita Beach Park

O. O. Denny Park
For a park map see
http://finnhillalliance.org
/wp-content/uploads/2012/09/
OO_Denny_Park_Trail_Guide.pdf

Watershed Park

City of Mercer Island Parks and Recreation

See www.mercergov.org/parks
and check Parks and Facilities
for the parks listed below.

Luther Burbank Park
(206) 275-7609

Mercerdale Park

Pioneer Park

City of Newcastle

May Creek Trail
www.newcastlewa.gov
/your_community/parks__trails
_and_other_recreation
/park_and_trail_maps

City of North Bend

Meadowbrook Farm
(425) 831-1900
www.meadowbrookfarm
preserve.org

Tollgate Farm Park
(425) 831-1900
www.siviewpark.org/tollgate
.phtml

City of Redmond

Farrel-McWhirter Farm Park
(425) 556-2300
www.redmond.gov
/ParksRecreation
/Farrel-McWhirterFarmPark

Redmond Watershed Preserve
(425) 556-2300
www.redmond.gov/cms/one
.aspx?portalId=169&pageId=4175

City of Sammamish Parks and Recreation

See www.sammamish.us/
parks-recreation/parks-trails
for parks listed below

Beaver Lake Preserve

Evans Creek Preserve

King County

Brightwater Center
www.kingcounty.gov/services
/environment/brightwater
-center.aspx

Metro King County Transit
http://kingcounty.gov/depts
/transportation/metro.aspx

Moss Lake Natural Area
www.kingcounty.gov/services
/environment/water-and-land
/natural-lands/ecological
/moss-lake.aspx

PSE Trail
(206) 477-4527
www.kingcounty.gov/services/gis
/Maps/vmc/Recreation.aspx

Rattlesnake Ledge and Mountain
www.seattle.gov/util
/EnvironmentConservation
/Education/CedarRiver
Watershed/RattlesnakeLedge
/index.htm

Ring Hill Forest
www.kingcounty.gov/services
/environment/water-and-land
/natural-lands/working
-resource-lands/ring-hill.aspx

Tolt Pipeline Trail
www.kingcountyexecutive
horsecouncil.org/trails/Tolt
Pipeline.htm

King County Parks
See www.kingcounty.gov
/services/parks-recreation
/parks and check the section
listed below.

Big Finn Hill Park
(206) 477-4527
See Trails, Backcountry Trails
on website.

Cougar Mountain Regional
Wildland Park
(206) 477-4527
See Parks and Natural Lands,
Popular Parks on website.

Cougar-Squak Corridor Park
(206) 477-4527
See Trails, Backcountry Trails
on website.

East Lake Sammamish Trail
See Trails, Regional Trails
on website.

Grand Ridge Park
(206) 477-4527
See Trails, Backcountry Trails
on website.

Marymoor Park
(206) 477-7275
See Parks and Natural Lands,
Popular Parks on website.

Preston-Snoqualmie Trail
See Trails, Regional Trails
on website.

Sammamish River Trail
See Trails, Regional Trails
on website.

Soaring Eagle Regional Park
(206) 477-4527
See Trails, Backcountry Trails
on website.

Snoqualmie Valley Trail
See Trails, Regional Trails
on website.

Taylor Mountain State Forest
See Trails, Backcountry Trails
on website.

Tolt River-John MacDonald Park
See Parks and Natural Lands,
Popular Parks on website.

Other

Campbell Global Forest and
Natural Resource Investment
www.sqrecreation.com
/snoqualmie/about/non
-motorized-recreation
-access-families/non
-motorized-recreation
-access-families

Puget Sound Energy
(Snoqualmie Falls Park)
https://pse.com/inyour
community/Toursand
Recreation/Pages
/Snoqualmie-Tours.aspx

Redmond Ridge Association
http://redmondridgeroa.com
/page/13210~102005/Maps

Washington Department of Natural Resources

Tiger Mountain
(206) 375-3558
www.dnr.wa.gov
/WestTigerMountain

Washington State Parks

See https://parks.state.wa.us for
the parks listed below.

Bridle Trails State Park
(425) 649-4275

Lake Sammamish State Park
(425) 649-4275

Saint Edward State Park
(425) 823-2992

Squak Mountain State Park
(425) 455-7010

TRAIL AND CONSERVATION ORGANIZATIONS

Bridle Trails Park Foundation
(425) 307-3578
www.bridletrails.org

Citizens for Saint Edward State Park
http://citizensforsaintedward
statepark.org/about

Friends of Marymoor Park
(206) 296-0673
http://marymoor.org

Forterra
http://forterra.org

Issaquah Alps Trails Club
http://issaquahalps.org

King County Parks Foundation
https://kingcountyparks
foundation.org

Kirkland Parks Foundation
(425) 298-4046
www.kirklandparks
foundation.org

Mountains to Sound Greenway
http://mtsgreenway.org

The Mountaineers
www.mountaineers.org

Nature Conservancy
www.nature.org

Newcastle Trails
www.newcastletrails.org

Trailhead Direct Shuttle
https://trailheaddirect.word
press.com/#post-50

Washington Wildlife and Recreation Coalition
www.wildliferecreation.org

Washington State Parks Foundation
http://wspf.org

Washington Trails Association
www.wta.org

RUNNING CLUBS AND ORGANIZED RUNS, HIKES, AND WALKS IN AND AROUND THE EASTSIDE

12Ks of Christmas

Popular Christmas-themed 12K (7.5 mile) run that utilizes the Cross Kirkland Corridor.
http://src12ksofchristmas.com

Beat the Blerch Runs

Fun-filled wacky race of various distances inspired by *The Oatmeal* comic strip and held at the Tolt River-John MacDonald Park.
www.beattheblerch.com

Bridle Trails Winter Running Festival

Popular and long-running January race that runs into the night. Festival includes 5-mile, 10-mile, 50K solo, 50K pair, and 50K relay races.
bridle.seattlerunning club.org

Cougar Mountain Trail Running Series

Very popular five-race trail running series at Cougar Mountain Regional Park sponsored by the Seattle Running Club. Series raises thousands of dollars for King County Parks each year.
https://cougar.seattlerunning club.org

Eastside Runners

Large and active running club open to all runners. Sponsors several fun runs and races.
www.eastsiderunners.com

Evergreen Trail Runs

Annual trail running races held at various Eastside parks, including Squak Mountain, Soaring Eagle Park, Tiger Mountain, Grand Ridge, Taylor Mountain, and East Lake Sammamish Trail.
http://evergreentrailruns.com

Issaquah Alps Trails Club

Issaquah-based conservation group that leads regular hikes in the surrounding Issaquah Alps and at other parks.
http://issaquahalps.org

Labor Day Half Marathon and Four Mile Walk

Long-running event partially held on the Sammamish River Trail.
http://labordayrun.com

Lake Washington Half Marathon

Course includes the Cross Kirkland Corridor.
http://lakewashingtonhalf.com

The Mountaineers

Seattle-based outdoors organization that has a Foothills Branch (based in Issaquah). They are involved with local conservation issues and also coordinate group outdoor activities.
www.mountaineers.org

Mount Si Relays and Ultra Runs

Well-established race sponsored by the Eastside Runners and held on the Snoqualmie Valley Trail.
www.mtsirelay.com

Northwest Trail Runs

Well-run series of trail runs that includes races at Redmond Watershed Park, Cougar Mountain Regional Park, Saint Edward State Park, Rattlesnake Ridge, and Lake Sammamish State Park.
http://nwtrailruns.com/events

Run for the Pies

Great family-friendly Fourth of July 5K held in Carnation. Course includes the Snoqualmie Valley Trail and trails within the Tolt River-John MacDonald County Park. Race awards are Remlinger Farm pies.
www.carnation4th.org/5k.html

Snoqualmie Valley Half

Large event that starts at the Tolt River-John MacDonald Park and heads out onto the Snoqualmie Valley Trail.
www.snoqualmievalleyrun.com

Virginia Mason Kirkland Mother's Day Half Marathon

Large and popular race utilizing the Cross Kirkland Corridor and trails through Juanita Bay Park.
http://promotionevents.com/md/index.php

INDEX

ABOUT THE AUTHOR

CRAIG ROMANO grew up in rural New Hampshire, where he fell in love with the natural world. He moved to Washington in 1989 and has since hiked more than 21,000 miles in the Evergreen State. An avid runner as well, Craig has run more than a hundred half marathons and twenty-five marathons and ultra runs, including the Boston Marathon, Mount Si 50K, and the White River 50 Mile Endurance Run.

Photo by Heather Romano

Craig is an award-winning author of more than twenty books; his *Columbia Highlands: Exploring Washington's Last Frontier* was recognized in 2010 by Washington secretary of state Sam Reed and state librarian Jan Walsh as a "Washington Reads" book for its contribution to Washington's cultural heritage. Craig also writes for numerous publications, tourism websites, and Hikeoftheweek.com.

When not hiking, running, and writing, he can be found napping with his wife, Heather; son, Giovanni; and cat, Giuseppe, at his home in Skagit County. Visit him at http://CraigRomano.com and on Facebook at "Craig Romano Guidebook Author."

MOUNTAINEERS BOOKS

recreation • lifestyle • conservation

MOUNTAINEERS BOOKS, including its two imprints, Skipstone and Braided River, is a leading publisher of quality outdoor recreation, sustainability, and conservation titles. As a 501(c)(3) nonprofit, we are committed to supporting the environmental and educational goals of our organization by providing expert information on human-powered adventure, sustainable practices at home and on the trail, and preservation of wilderness.

Our publications are made possible through the generosity of donors, and through sales of more than 800 titles on outdoor recreation, sustainable lifestyle, and conservation. To donate, purchase books, or learn more, visit us online:

MOUNTAINEERS BOOKS

1001 SW Klickitat Way, Suite 201 • Seattle, WA 98134
800-553-4453 • mbooks@mountaineersbooks.org
www.mountaineersbooks.org

An independent nonprofit publisher since 1960

OTHER TITLES AVAILABLE FROM MOUNTAINEERS BOOKS:

Mountaineers Books is proud to support the Leave No Trace Center for Outdoor Ethics, whose mission is to promote and inspire responsible outdoor recreation through education, research, and partnerships. The Leave No Trace program is focused specifically on human-powered (nonmotorized) recreation. For more information, visit www.lnt.org.